Piano • Vocal • Guitar

THE BEST BIG BAND SONGS EVER

4th Edition

The
BEST
BIG
BAND
SONGS
Ever

ISBN 978-1-5400-4144-9

Visit Hal Leonard Online at
www.halleonard.com

Contact us:
Hal Leonard
7777 West Bluemound Road
Milwaukee, WI 53213
Email: info@halleonard.com

In Europe, contact:
Hal Leonard Europe Limited
42 Wigmore Street
Marylebone, London, W1U 2RN
Email: info@halleonardeurope.com

In Australia, contact:
Hal Leonard Australia Pty. Ltd.
4 Lentara Court
Cheltenham, Victoria, 3192 Australia
Email: info@halleonard.com.au

CONTENTS

ACROSS THE ALLEY FROM THE ALAMO

Words and Music by
JOE GREENE

pin - to spent his time a - swish - in' flies___ and the Na - va - jo watched the
thought that they would make some eas - y bucks___ if they're wash - in' their fri - jo - les in

la - zy skies,___ and ver - y rare - ly did they ev - er rest their eyes___ on the
Duz and Lux,___ a pair of ver - y con - sci - en - tious clucks___ to the

peo - ple pass - ing by._____ One day, they went a -
peo - ple pass - ing by._____ Then they took this cheap va -

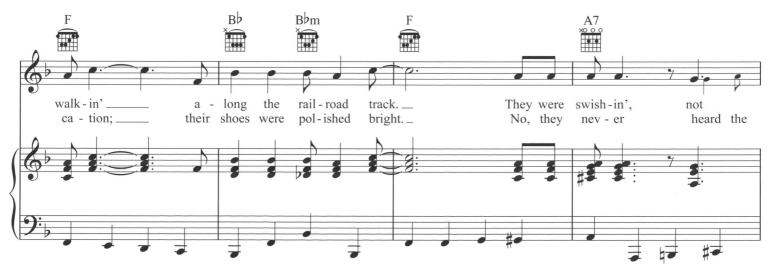

walk - in'_____ a - long the rail - road track.___ They were swish - in', not
ca - tion;_____ their shoes were pol - ished bright._ No, they nev - er heard the

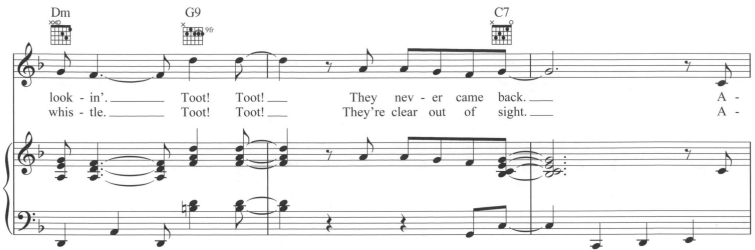

look - in'. _____ Toot! Toot! ___ They nev - er came back. ___ A -
whis - tle. _____ Toot! Toot! ___ They're clear out of sight. ___ A -

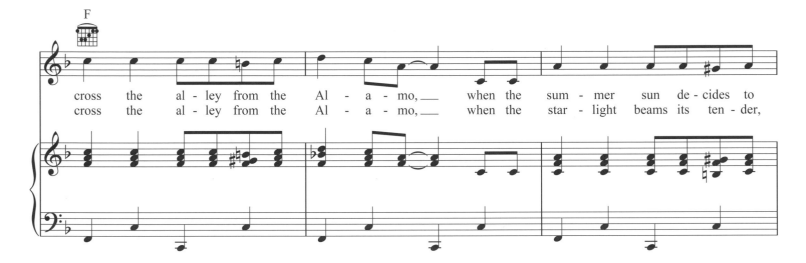

cross the al - ley from the Al - a - mo, ___ when the sum - mer sun de - cides to
cross the al - ley from the Al - a - mo, ___ when the star - light beams its ten - der,

set - tle low, ___ a fly sings an In - di - an hi - de - ho ___ to the
ten - der glow, ___ the beams go to sleep and there ain't no dough ___ for the

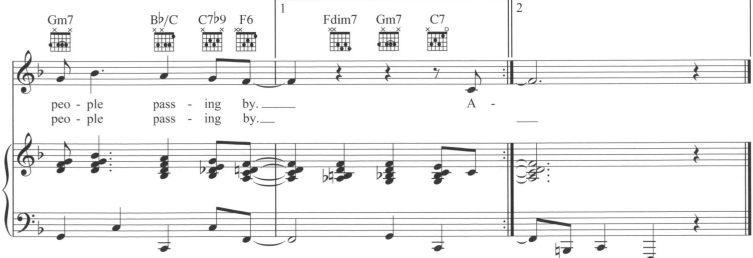

peo - ple pass - ing by. _____   A -
peo - ple pass - ing by. ___

ALRIGHT, OKAY, YOU WIN

Words and Music by SID WYCHE
and MAYME WATTS

Moderately, with rhythm

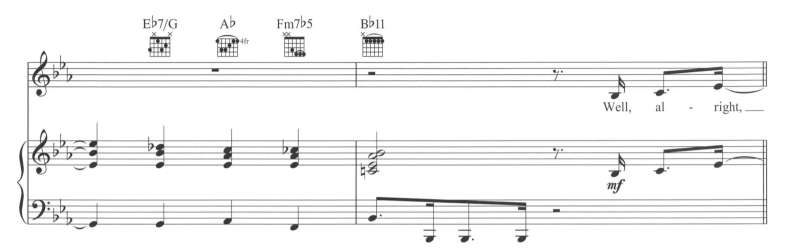

Well, al - right, ___

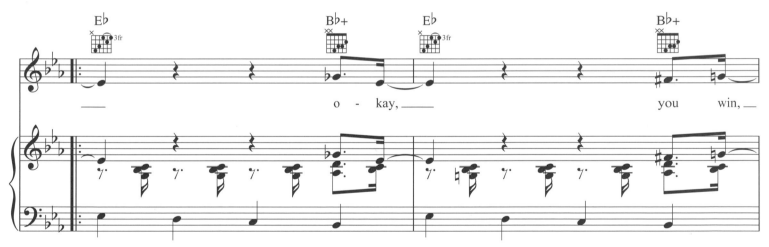

___ o - kay, ___ you win, ___

___ I'm in love with you. ___ Well, al - right, ___

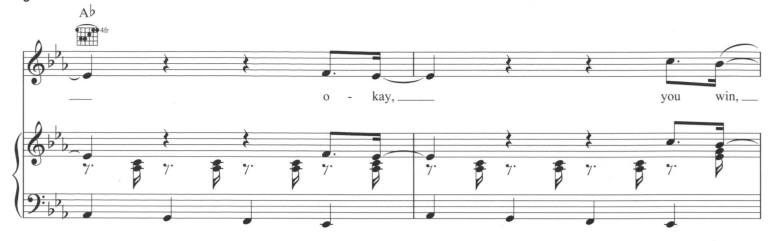

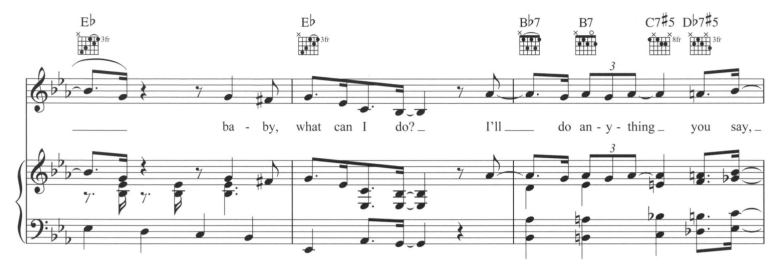

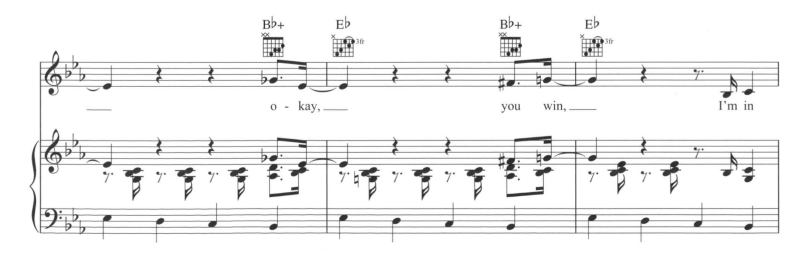

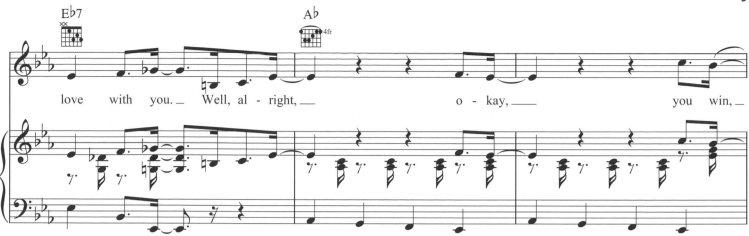

love with you.___ Well, al - right, ___ o - kay, ___ you win, ___

___ Ba - by, what can I do? ___ An - y-thing you say ___ I'll do, ___

___ as long as it's me and you. ___

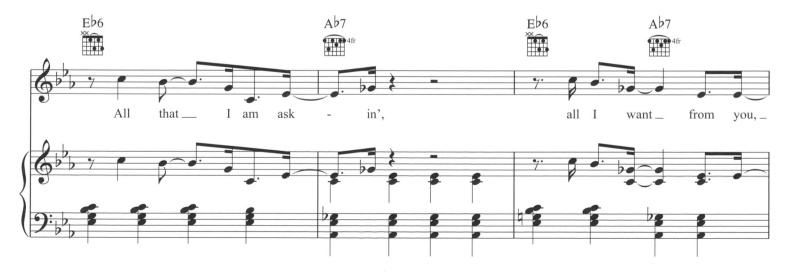

All that ___ I am ask - in', all I want ___ from you, ___

just love —— me like I love —— you an' it

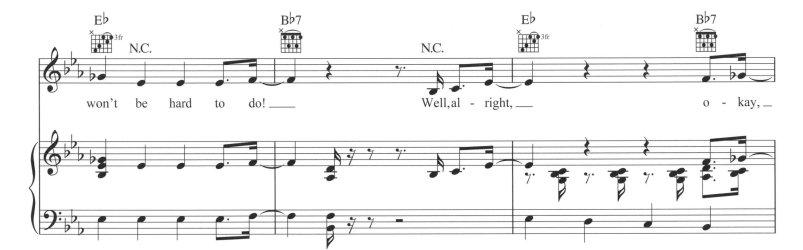

won't be hard to do! —— Well, al - right, —— o - kay, ——

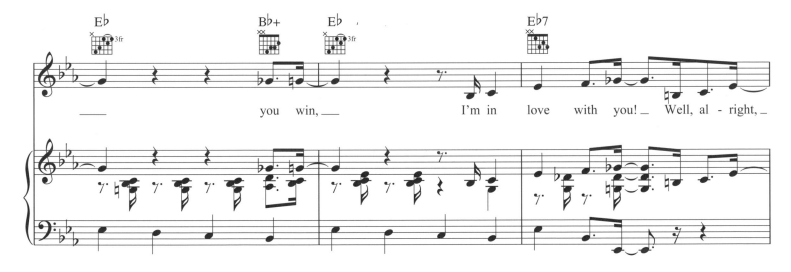

—— you win, —— I'm in love with you! —— Well, al - right, ——

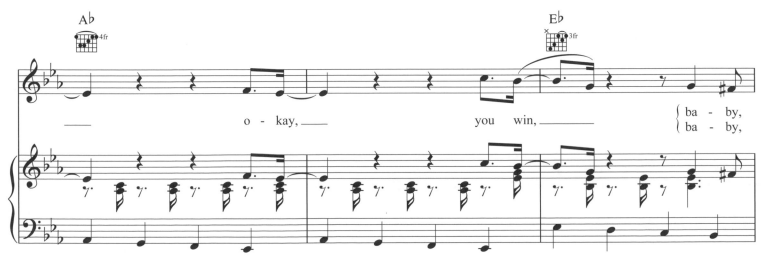

—— o - kay, —— you win, —————— { ba - by, { ba - by,

what can I do? ___ I'll ___ do an - y - thing ___ you say. ___ It's
one thing more, _ if ___ you're gon - na be ___ my man, _

just got to be that way. ___ Well, al - right, _ ___ sweet ba -

- by, take me by the hand. ___ Well, al - right, _ ___ o - kay, _

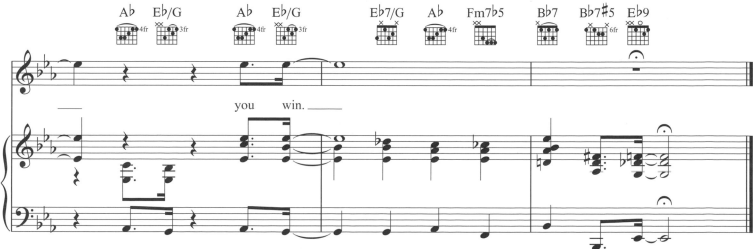

___ you win. ___

APRIL IN PARIS

Words by E.Y. "YIP" HARBURG
Music by VERNON DUKE

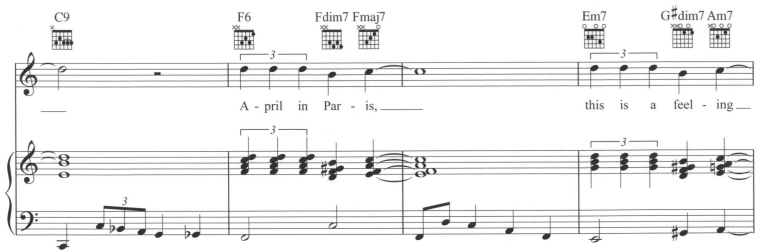

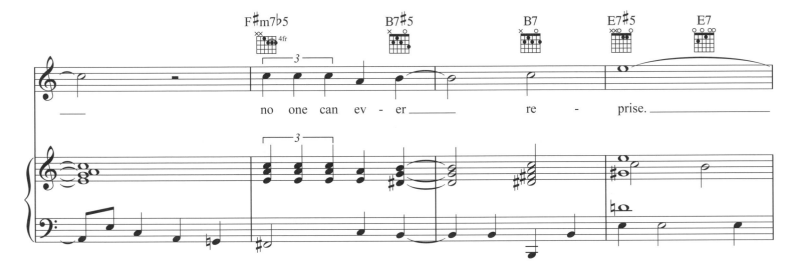

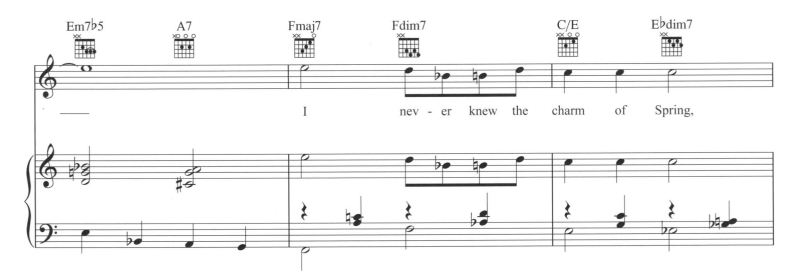

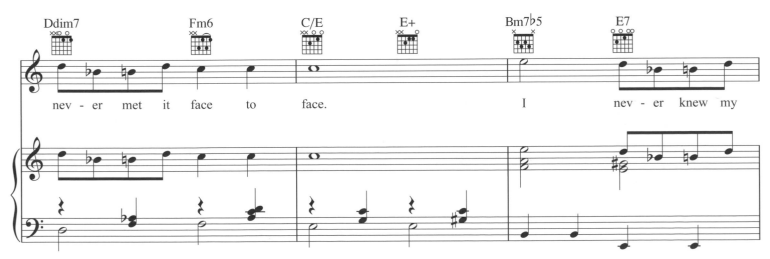

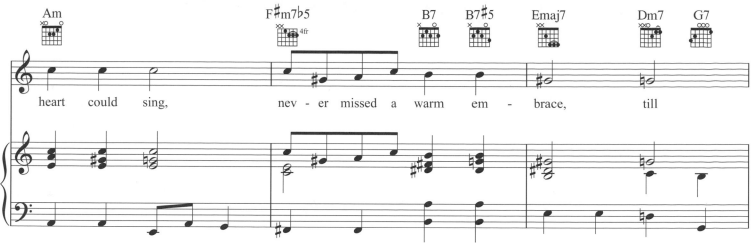

heart could sing, never missed a warm em - brace, till

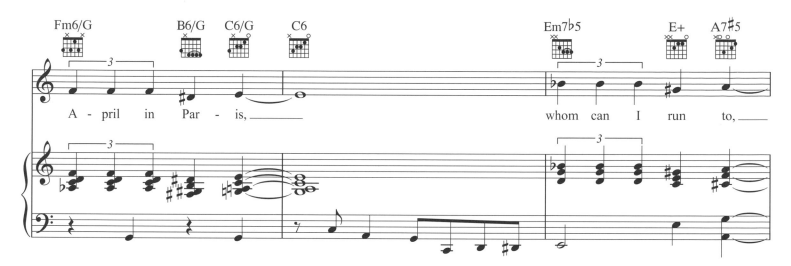

A - pril in Par - is, whom can I run to,

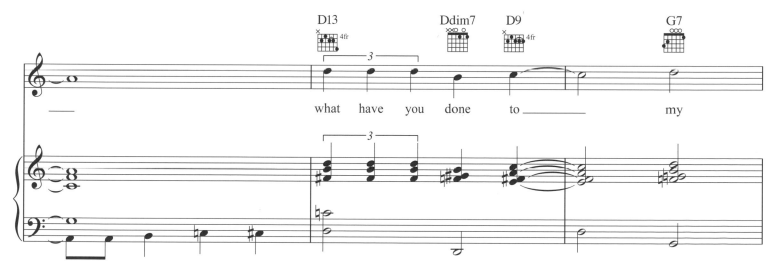

what have you done to my

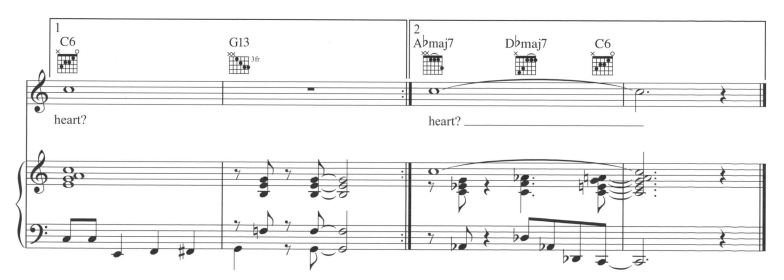

heart? | heart?

AQUELLOS OJOS VERDES
(Green Eyes)

Music by NILO MENENDEZ
Spanish Words by ADOLFO UTRERA
English Words by E. RIVERA and E. WOODS

Moderately

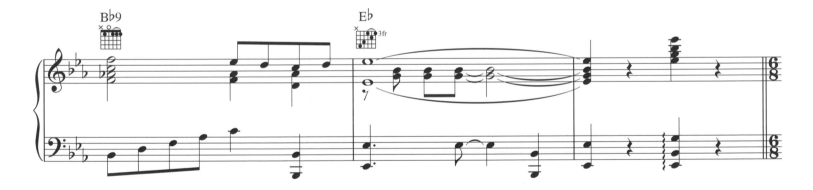

Life held no charm, dear, un-til I met you.
Fue - ron tus o - jos los que me die - rón

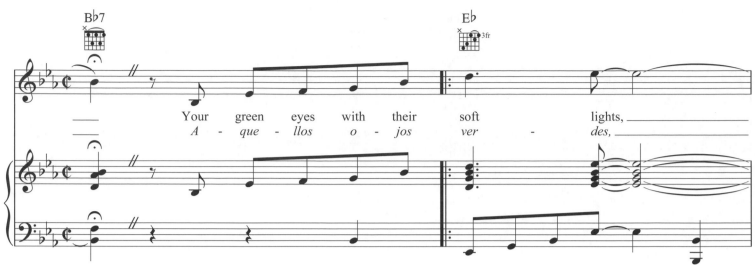

Your green eyes with their soft lights,_____
A - que - llos o - jos ver - des,_____

your eyes that prom - ise sweet nights_____ bring to my soul a
de mi - ra - da se - re - na_____ De - ja - ron en mi

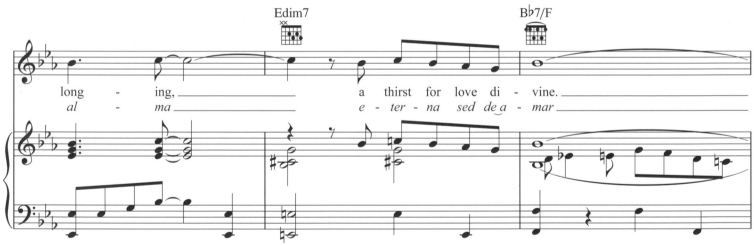

long - ing,_____ a thirst for love di - vine._____
al - ma_____ e - ter - na sed de a - mar_____

In dreams I seem to hold you,_____ to find you and en -
An - be - los de ca - ri - cias_____ de be - sos y ter -

fold you,_____ our lips meet, and our hearts, too,_____
nu - ras _____ de to - das las dul - zu - ras _____

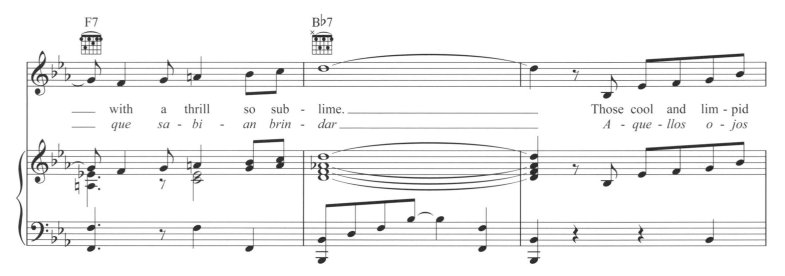

__ with a thrill so sub - lime._____ Those cool and lim - pid
__ que sa - bi - an brin - dar _____ A - que - llos o - jos

green eyes,_____ a pool where in my love lies _____
ver - des _____ se - re - nos co - mo un la - go

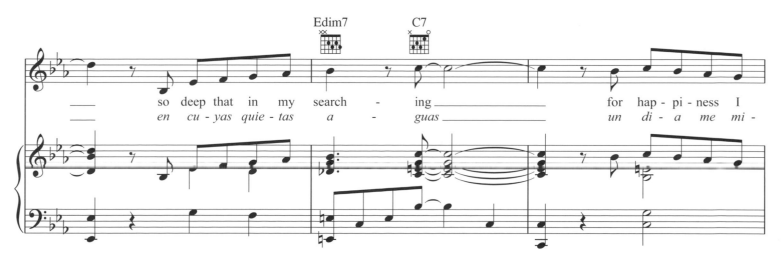

__ so deep that in my search - ing _____ for hap - pi - ness I
__ en cu - yas quie - tas a - guas _____ un di - a me mi-

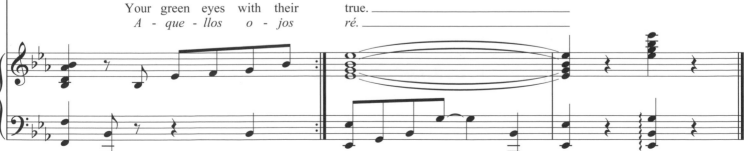

BASIN STREET BLUES

Words and Music by
SPENCER WILLIAMS

lan' of dreams, __ you'll nev-er know how nice it seems or just how much it real-ly means.

Glad to be, __ yes, sir-ee, __ where wel-come's free, __

dear to me, __ where I can lose __ my Ba-sin Street blues. __

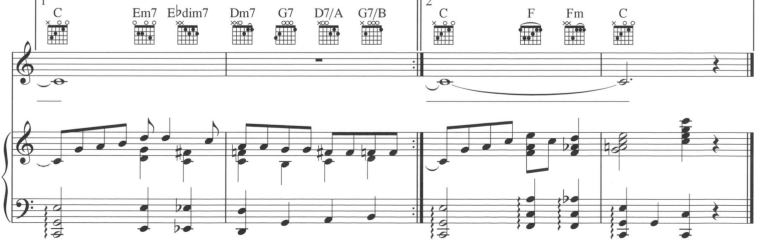

BEGIN THE BEGUINE

from JUBILEE

Words and Music by
COLE PORTER

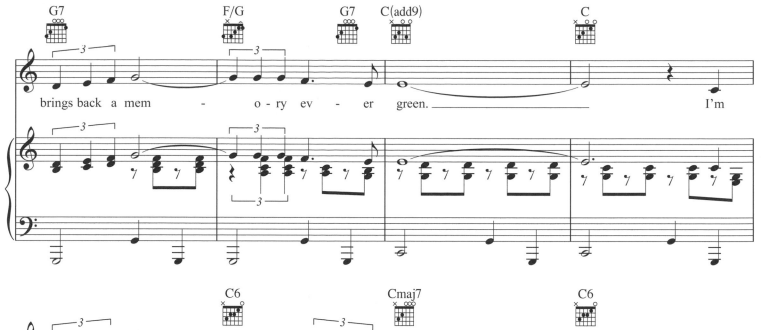

brings back a mem - o - ry ev - er green. _____ I'm

with you once more _____ un - der the stars, _____ and

down by the shore _____ an or - ches - tra's play - ing, _____ and

e - ven the palms _____ seem to be sway - ing _____

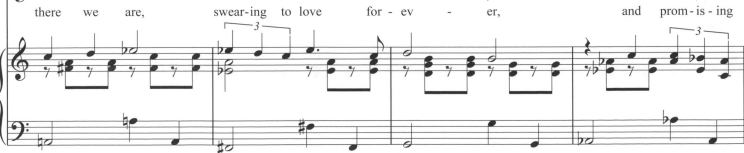

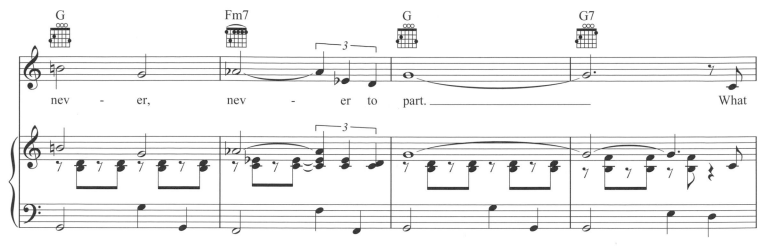

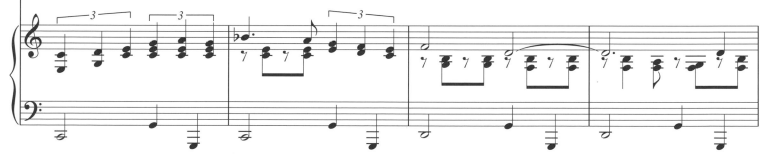

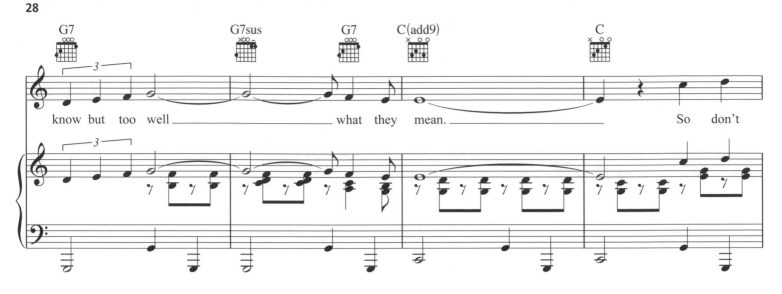

know but too well _____ what they mean. _____ So don't

let them be - gin _____ the Be - guine. _____ Let the

love that was once a fire re-main an em - ber. _____ Let it

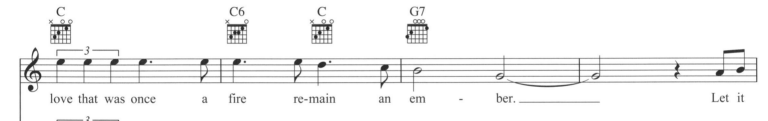

sleep like the dead de - sire I on - ly re - mem - ber _____

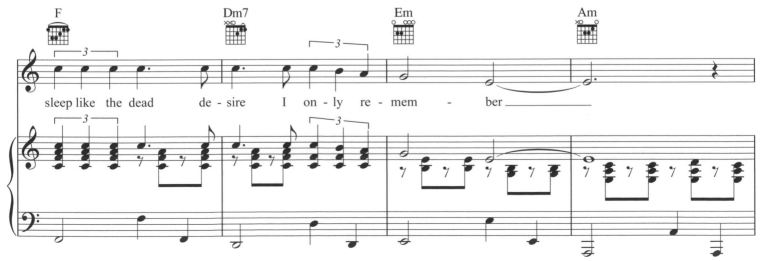

sud-den-ly know _____ what heav-en we're in _____

when they be - gin _____ the Be - guine, _____

when they be - gin _____ the Be-

guine. _____

CANDY

Words and Music by MACK DAVID,
ALEX KRAMER and JOAN WHITNEY

stands me, my un-der-stand-ing Can - dy

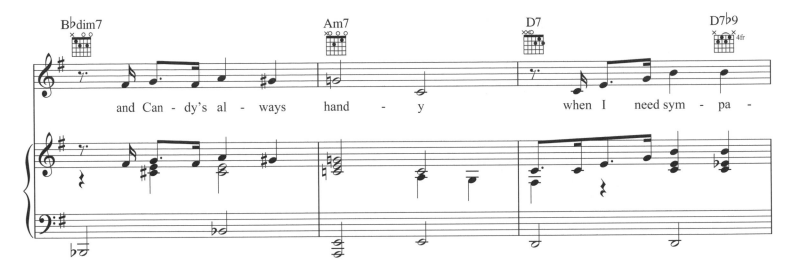

and Can-dy's al-ways hand-y when I need sym-pa -

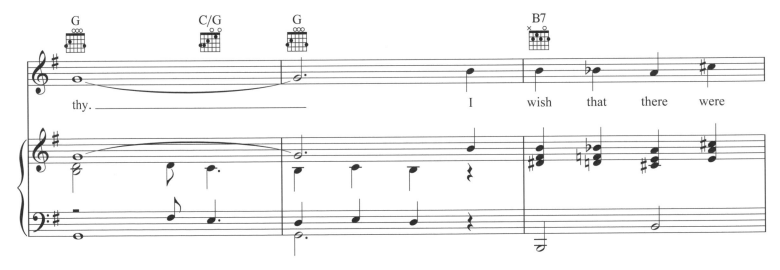

thy. _____ I wish that there were

four of {him / her} so I could love much more of {him. / her.}

BOOGIE WOOGIE BUGLE BOY

from BUCK PRIVATES

Words and Music by DON RAYE
and HUGHIE PRINCE

Medium Boogie Woogie

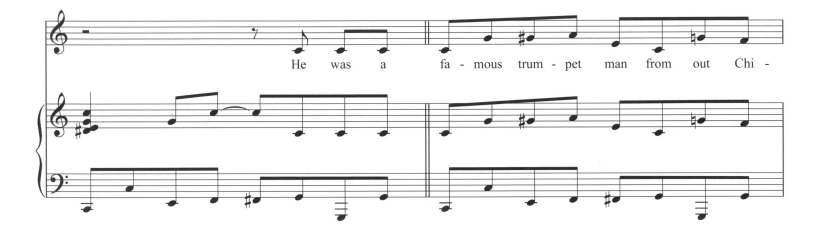

He was a fa-mous trum-pet man from out Chi-

ca-go way, ___ he had a "boo-gie" style that no one

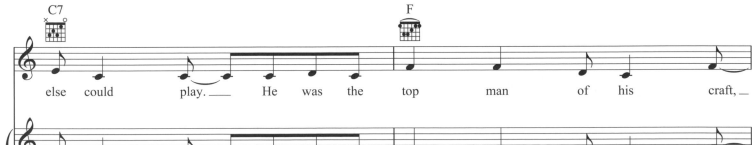

else could play. ___ He was the top man of his craft, ___

BYE BYE BLACKBIRD

from PETE KELLY'S BLUES

Words by MORT DIXON
Music by RAY HENDERSON

black - bird, gotta be on my way,
blue - bird, this is my luck - y day,

where there's sun - shine ga - lore.
now my dreams will come true.

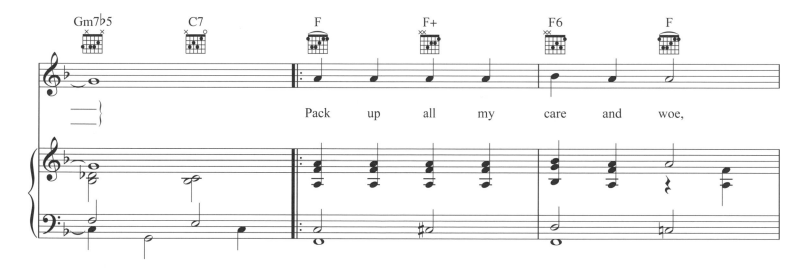

Pack up all my care and woe,

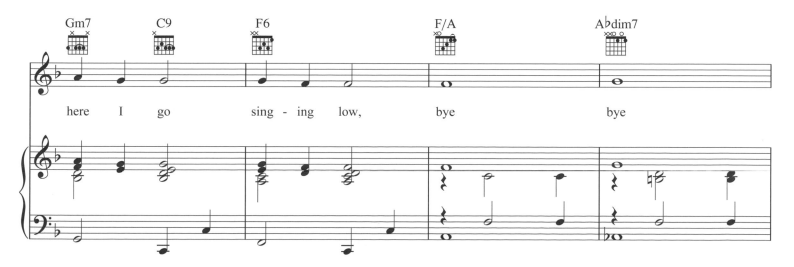

here I go sing - ing low, bye bye

black - bird. _____ Where some - bod - y

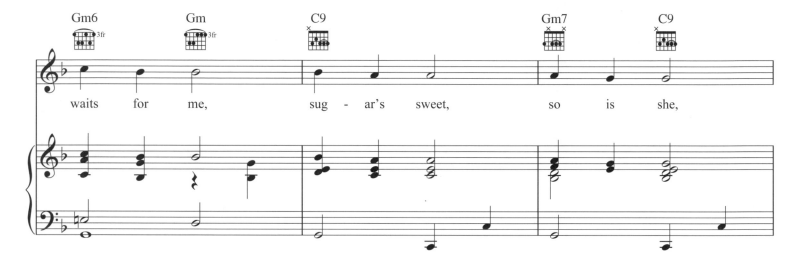

waits for me, sug - ar's sweet, so is she,

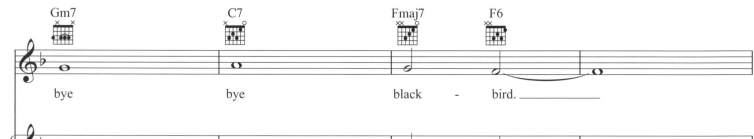

bye bye black - bird. _____

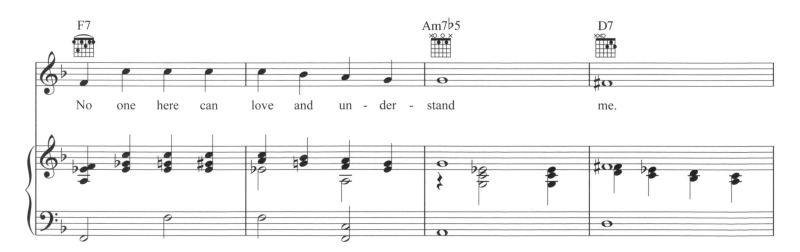

No one here can love and un - der - stand me.

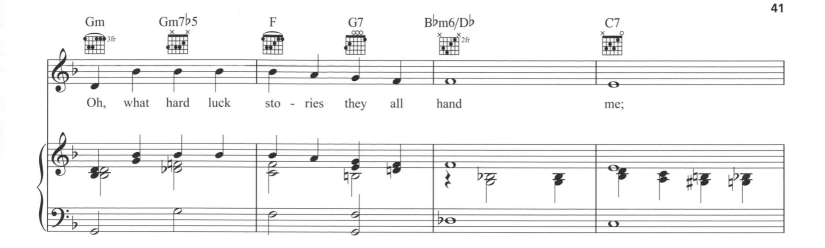

Oh, what hard luck sto - ries they all hand me;

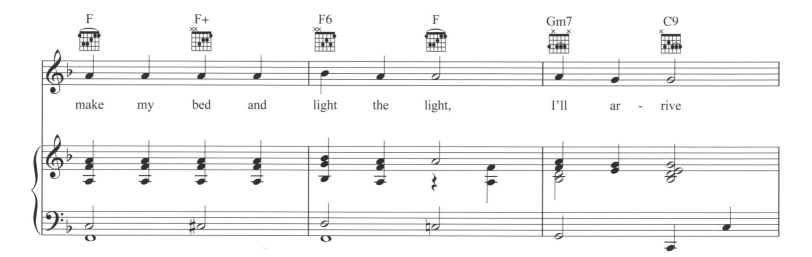

make my bed and light the light, I'll ar - rive

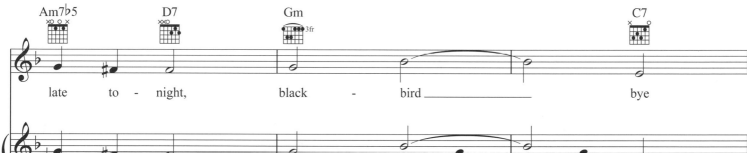

late to - night, black - bird _____ bye

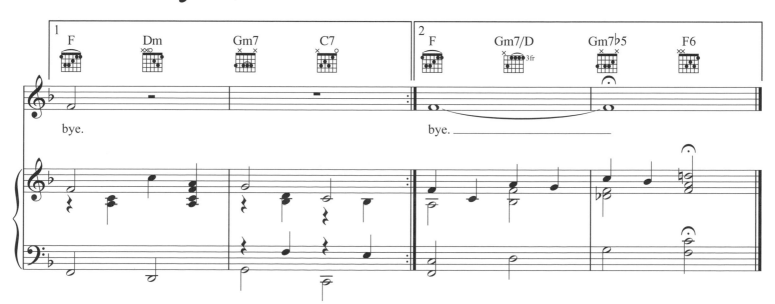

bye.

bye. _____

CALDONIA
(What Makes Your Big Head So Hard?)

Words and Music by
FLEECIE MOORE

Medium Boogie-Woogie

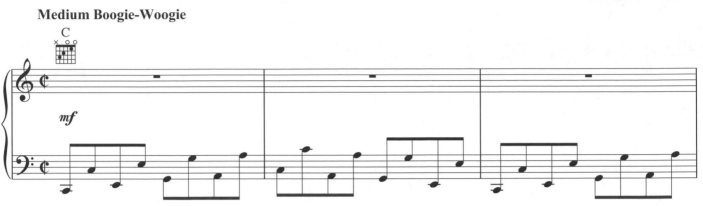

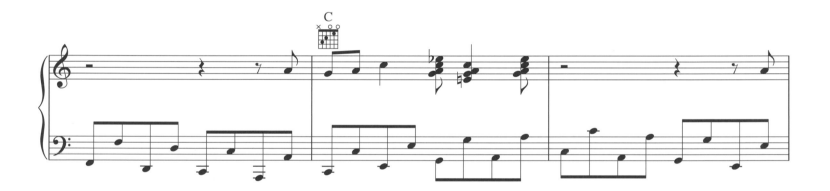

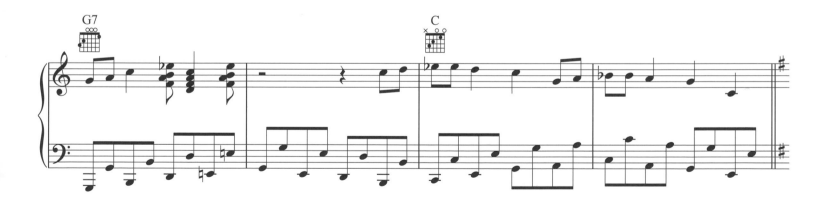

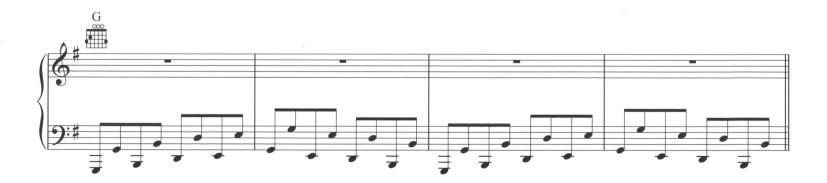

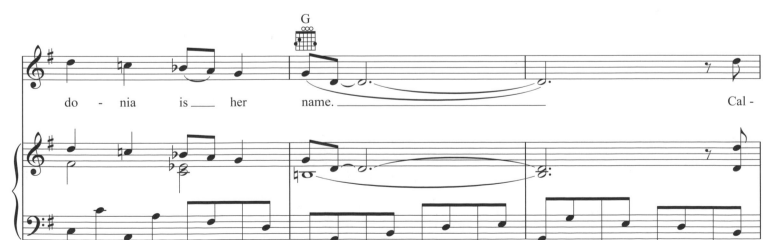

(Spoken:) My mama told me to leave Caldonia alone: "She's bad for your morale."

But mama didn't know I loved Caldonia. She's

C9

G D9(add11)

such a swell gal! So, I'm goin' down to

D7 G

Caldonia's house and ask her just one more time. Cal-

do - nia!　　　　Cal - do - nia!　　　　What makes your big head so　hard?

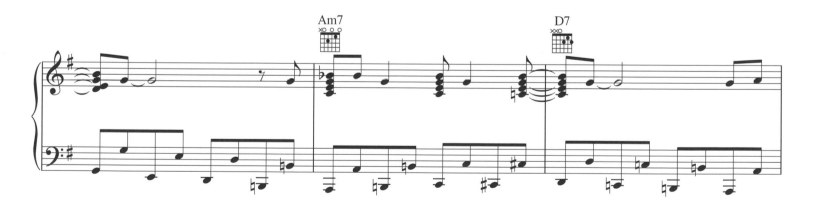

CARAVAN

Words and Music by DUKE ELLINGTON,
IRVING MILLS and JUAN TIZOL

on our car - a - van. _____

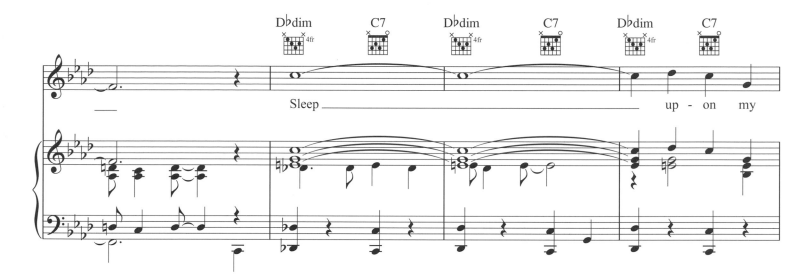

_____ Sleep _____ up - on my

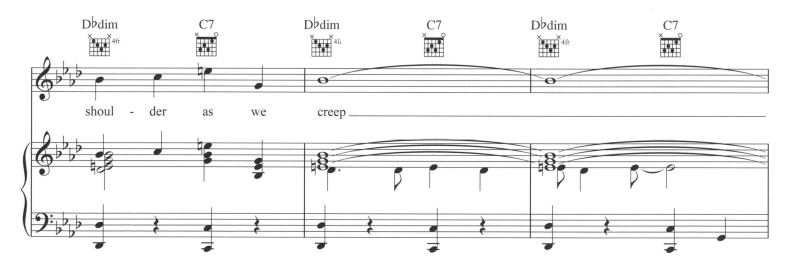

shoul - der as we creep _____

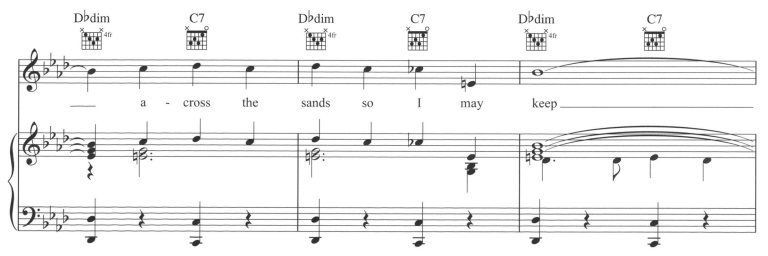

_____ a - cross the sands so I may keep _____

this mem - 'ry of our car - a -

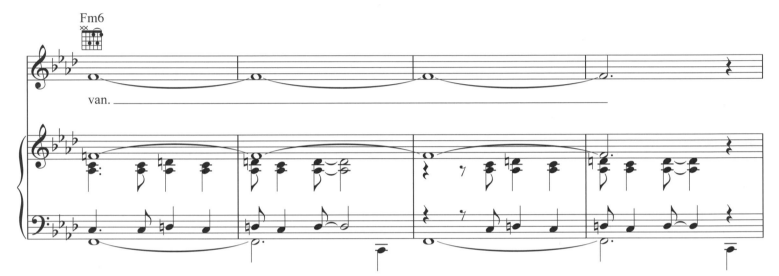

van.

This _____ is so ex - cit - ing

you _____ are so in - vit -

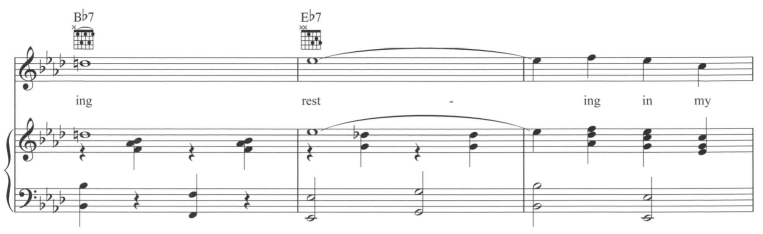

ing rest - ing in my

arms as I thrill to _____

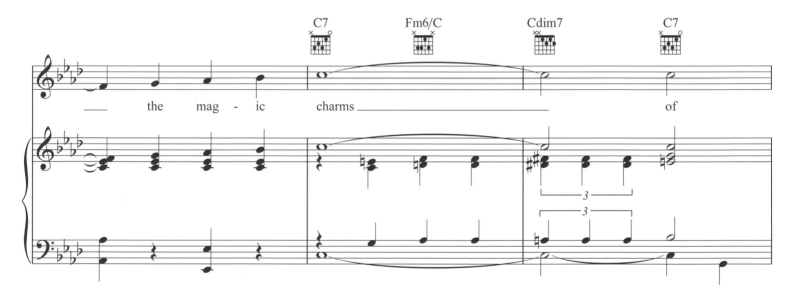

_____ the mag - ic charms _____ of

you, _____ Be - side me

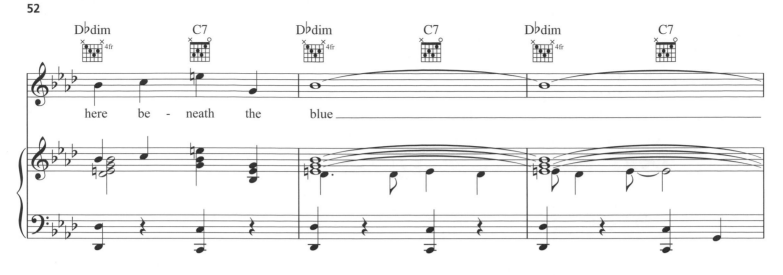

here be - neath the blue

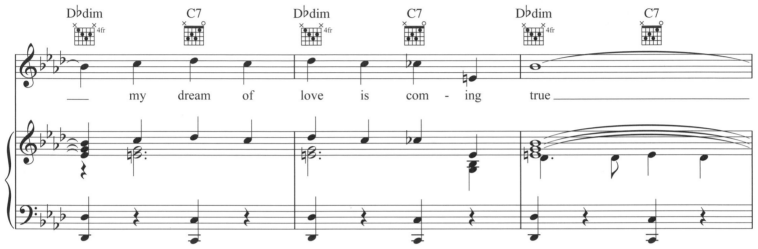

my dream of love is com - ing true

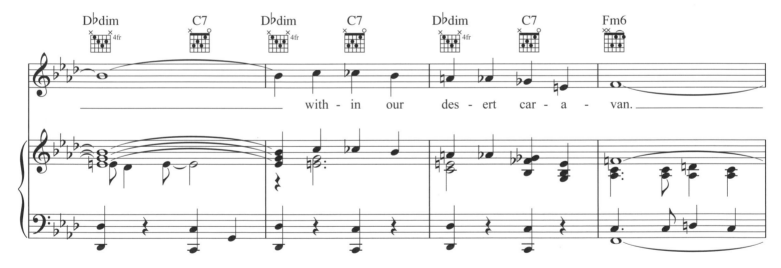

with - in our des - ert car - a - van.

CHATTANOOGA CHOO CHOO

Words by MACK GORDON
Music by HARRY WARREN

I can af-ford _____ to board a Chat-ta-noo-ga Choo-Choo, _____

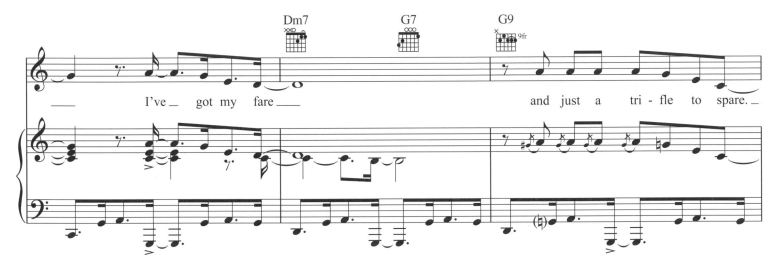

_____ I've_ got my fare _____ and just a tri-fle to spare.

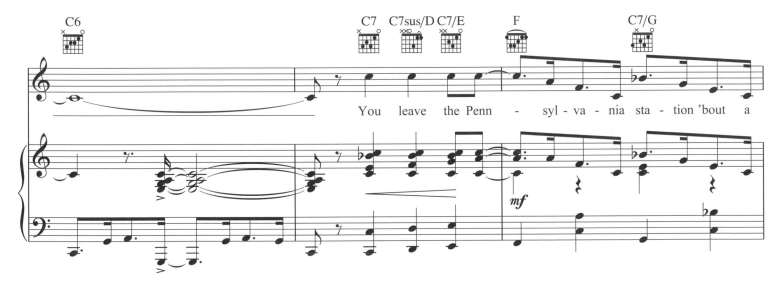

_____ You leave the Penn - syl-va-nia sta-tion 'bout a

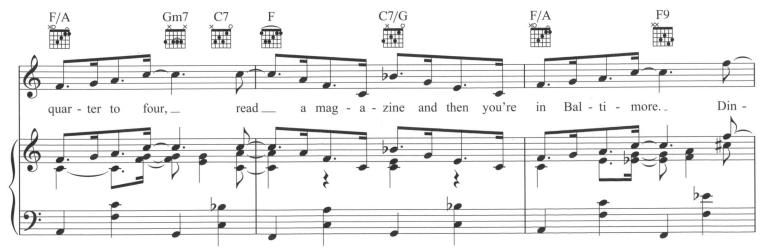

quar-ter to four,_ read_ a mag-a-zine and then you're in Bal-ti-more. Din-

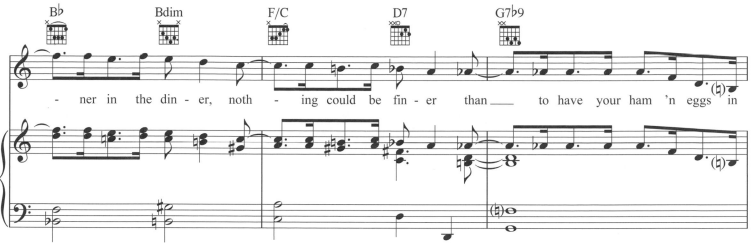

-ner in the din-er, noth-ing could be fin-er than ___ to have your ham 'n eggs in

Car-o-li-na. When ___ you hear the whis-tle blow-in' eight to the bar ___ then ___

___ you know that Ten-nes-see is not ver-y far, ___ shov-el all the coal in, got-

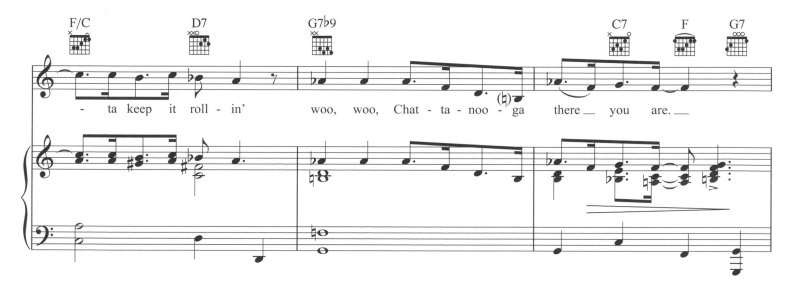

-ta keep it roll-in' woo, woo, Chat-ta-noo-ga there ___ you are. ___

There's gon - na be _____

_____ a cer - tain par - ty at the sta - tion _____ sat - in and lace, _____

_____ I used to call fun - ny face. _____

She's gon - na cry _____ un - til I tell her that I'll

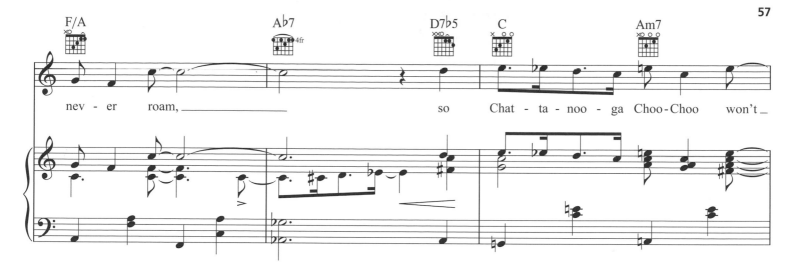

never roam, _____ so Chat - ta - noo - ga Choo-Choo won't _

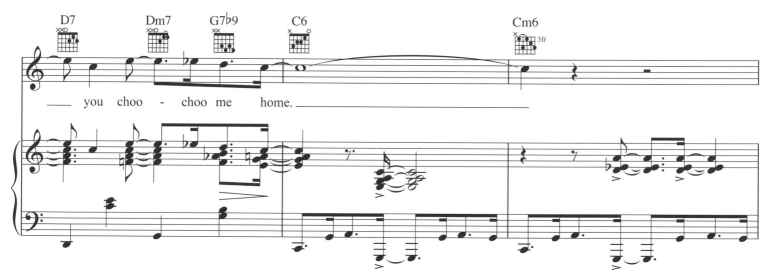

_____ you choo - choo me home. _____

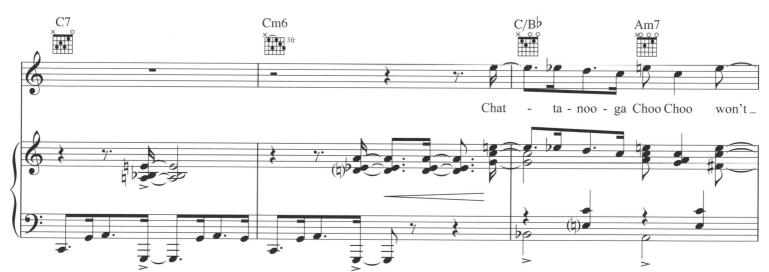

Chat - ta - noo - ga Choo Choo won't _

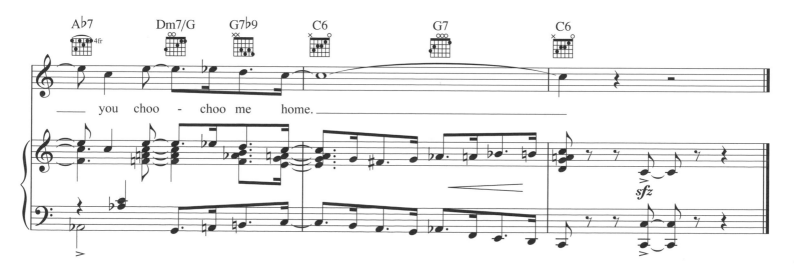

_____ you choo - choo me home. _____

CHEROKEE
(Indian Love Song)

Words and Music by
RAY NOBLE

Moderately bright Swing

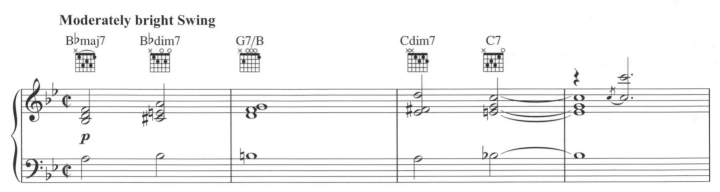

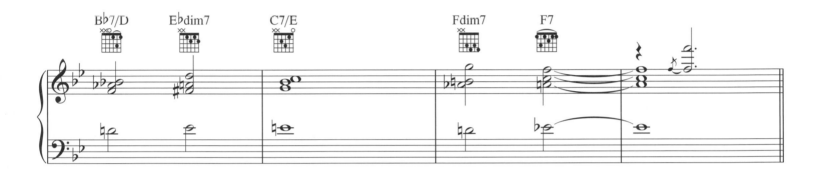

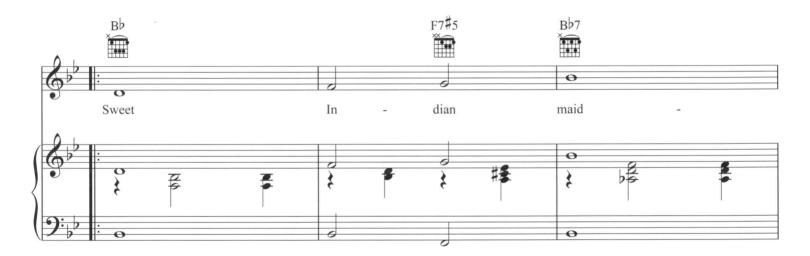

Sweet In - dian maid -

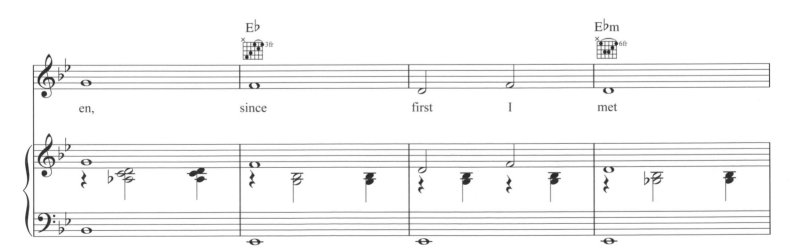

en, since first I met

you, I can't for - get

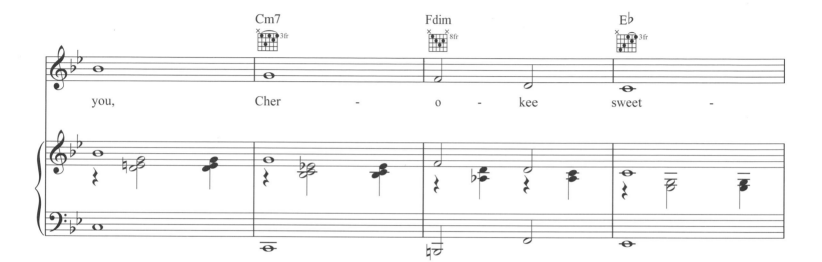

you, Cher - o - kee sweet -

heart. Child of the prai -

rie, your love keeps call -

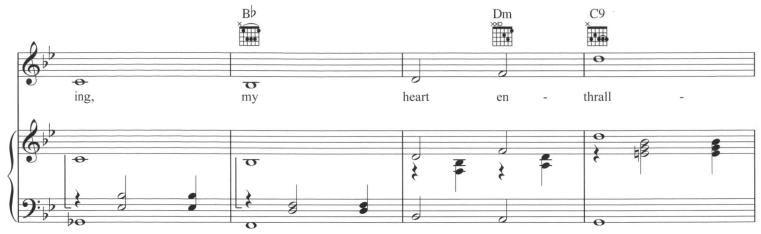

ing, my heart en - thrall -

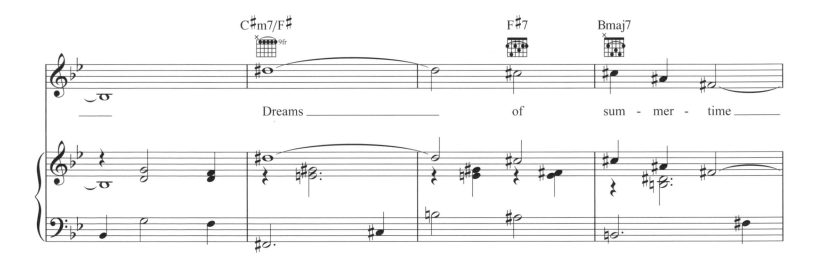

ing, Cher - o - kee.

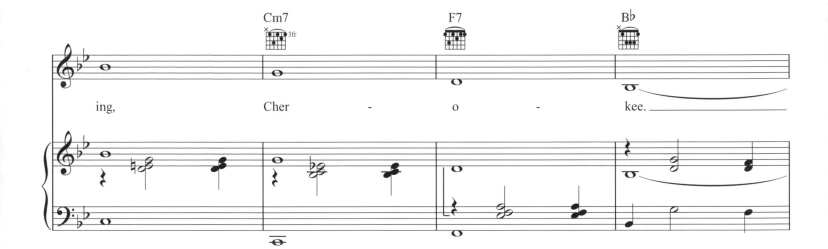

Dreams of sum - mer - time

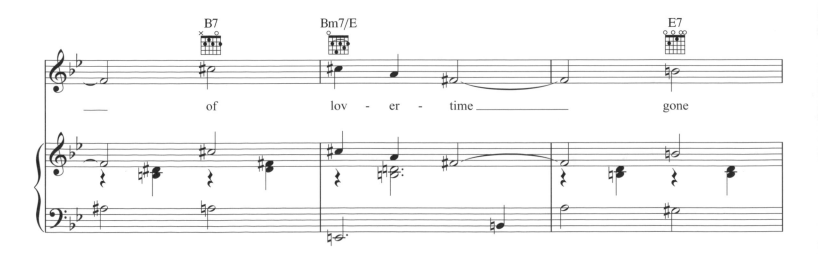

of lov - er - time gone

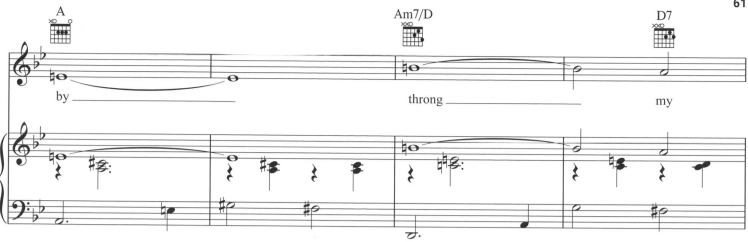

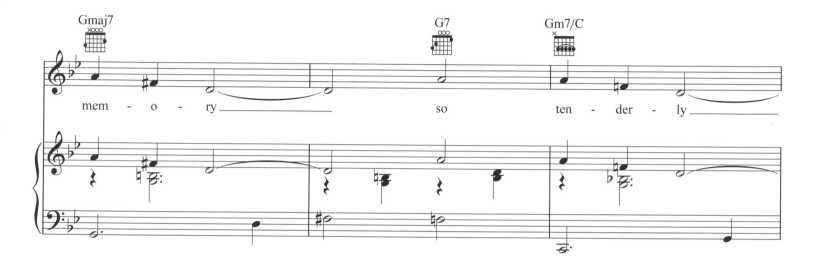

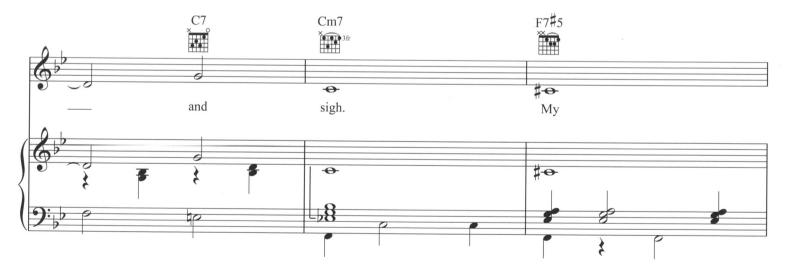

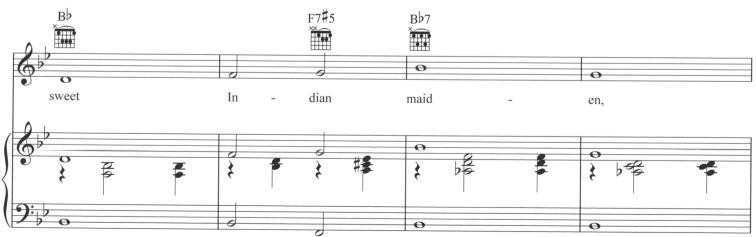

one   day   I'll   hold   you,

in   my   arms   fold   you,

Cher - o - kee.

kee.

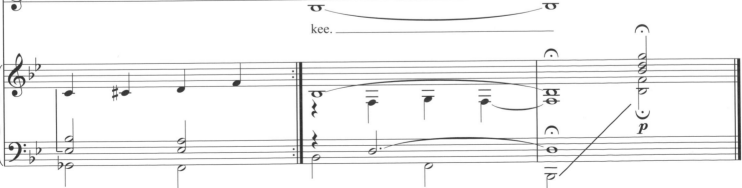

DADDY

Words and Music by
BOB TROUP

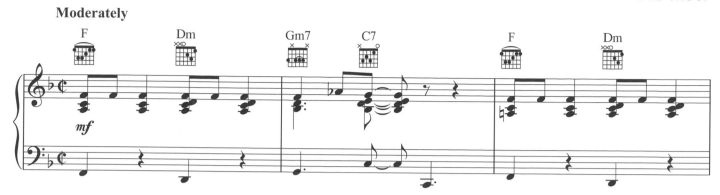

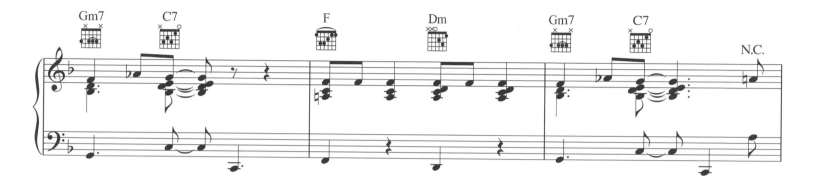

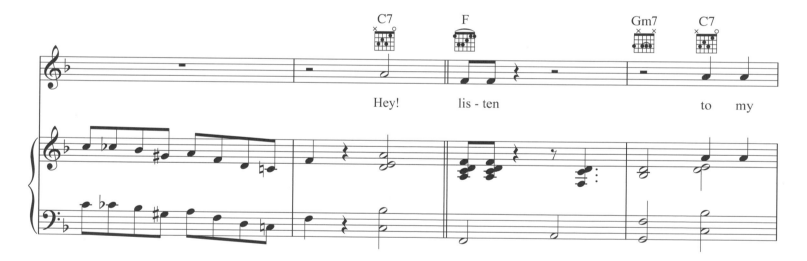

Hey! lis-ten to my

sto-ry 'bout ___ a gal named Dai-sy Mae, ___

64

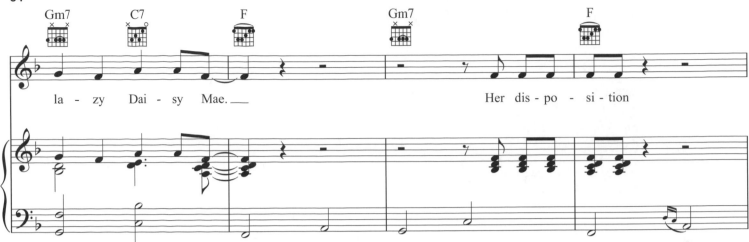

la - zy Dai - sy Mae. ___ Her dis - po - si - tion

is rath - er sweet and charm - ing; at times a - larm - ing,

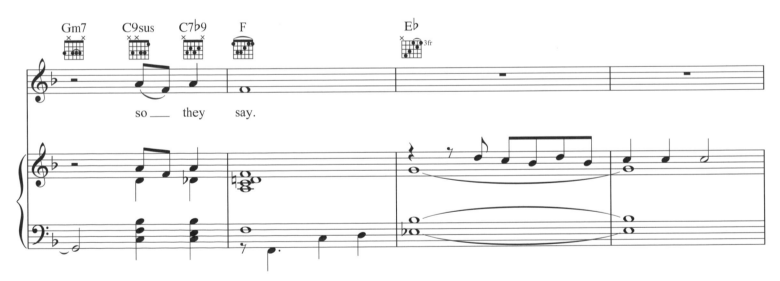

so ___ they say.

She had a man; rich, tall, dark, hand-some,

large and strong — to whom she used to sing this song: — Hey!

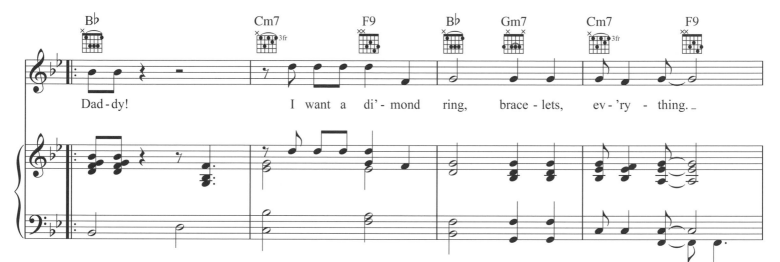

Dad-dy! I want a di'-mond ring, brace-lets, ev-'ry-thing. —

Dad-dy! You ought-a get the best for me. — Hey!

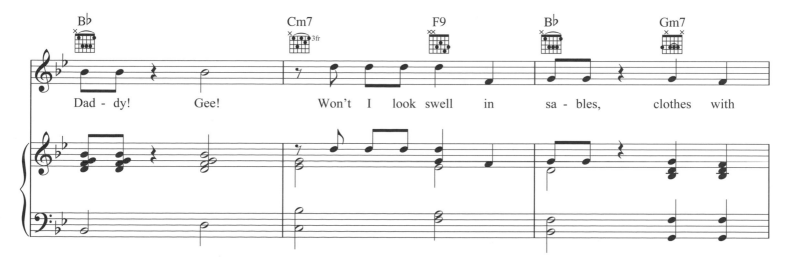

Dad-dy! Gee! Won't I look swell in sa-bles, clothes with

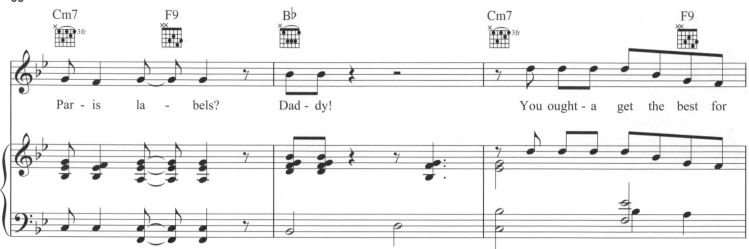

Par - is la - bels? Dad - dy! You ought - a get the best for

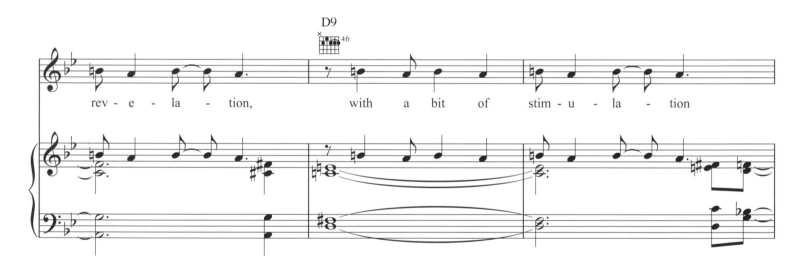

me. _____ Here's 'n a - maz - ing

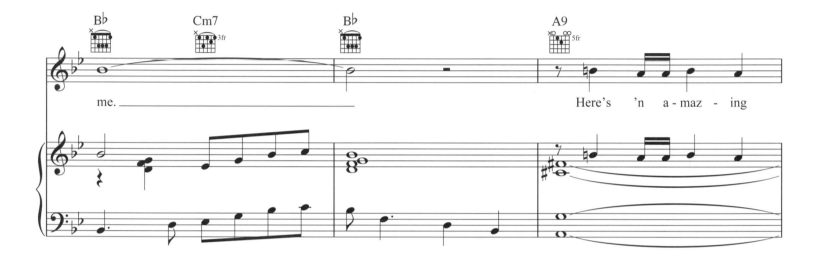

rev - e - la - tion, with a bit of stim - u - la - tion

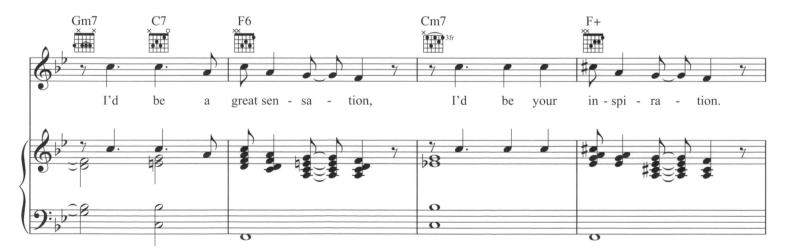

I'd be a great sen - sa - tion, I'd be your in - spi - ra - tion.

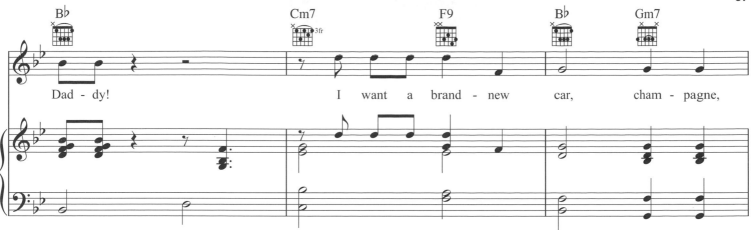

Daddy! I want a brand-new car, champagne,

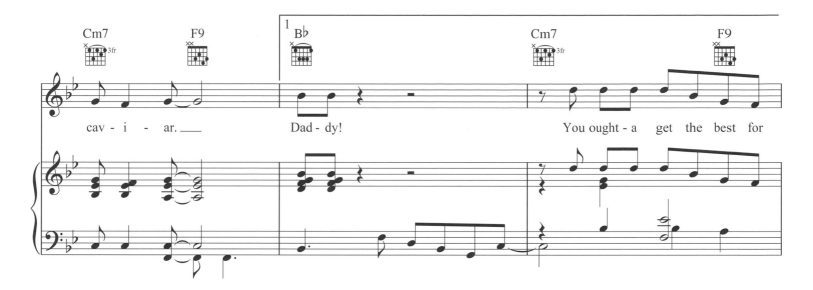

caviar. Daddy! You oughta get the best for

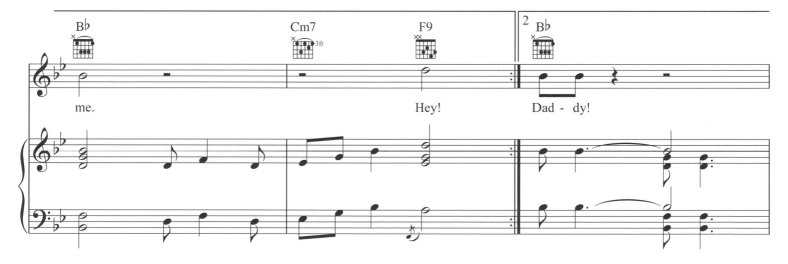

me. Hey! Daddy!

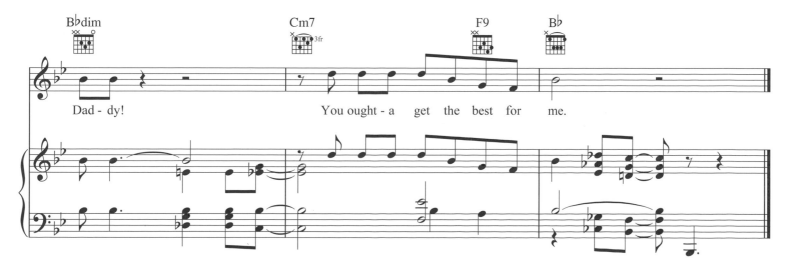

Daddy! You oughta get the best for me.

CIRIBIRIBIN

Based on the original melody by A. PESTALOZZA
English version by HARRY JAMES,
JACK LAWRENCE, PATTI ANDREWS,
MAXENE ANDREWS and LAVERNE ANDREWS

Moderate Swing

Ci - ri - bi - ri - bin, he waits for her each night be-

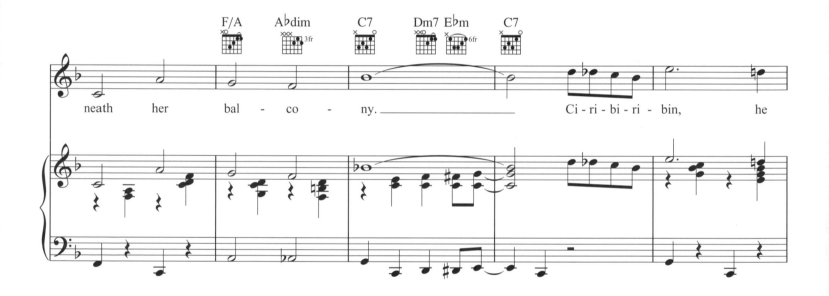

neath her bal - co - ny. _____ Ci - ri - bi - ri - bin, he

begs to hold her tight but, no, she _____ won't a - gree.

Ci - ri - bi - ri - bin, she throws a rose and

blows a kiss from up a - bove. _____ Ci - ri - bi - ri -

bin, _____ Ci - ri - bi - ri - bin, _____ Ci - ri - bi - ri - bin, they're

so in love. _____ Ci - ri - bi - ri - love. _____

DON'T BE THAT WAY

Words and Music by BENNY GOODMAN,
MITCHELL PARISH and EDGAR SAMPSON

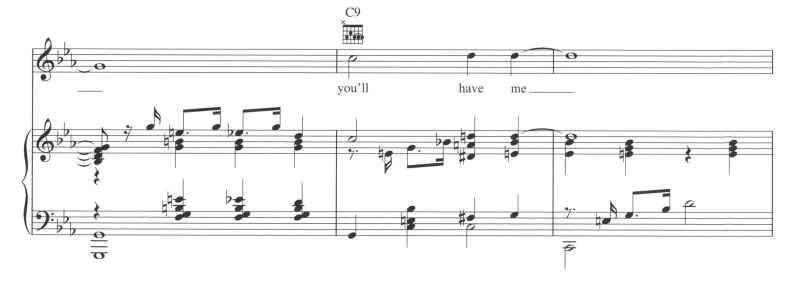

(I Love You)
FOR SENTIMENTAL REASONS

Words by DEEK WATSON
Music by WILLIAM BEST

I love you _____ for sen - ti - men - tal rea - sons. _____ I hope you do be - lieve me; _____ I'll give you my heart. _____ I

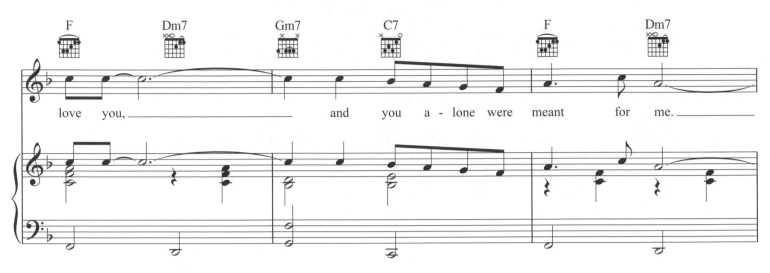

love you, _____ and you a-lone were meant for me. _____

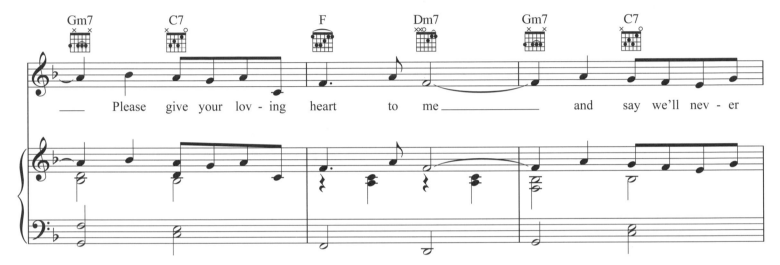

___ Please give your lov-ing heart to me _____ and say we'll nev-er

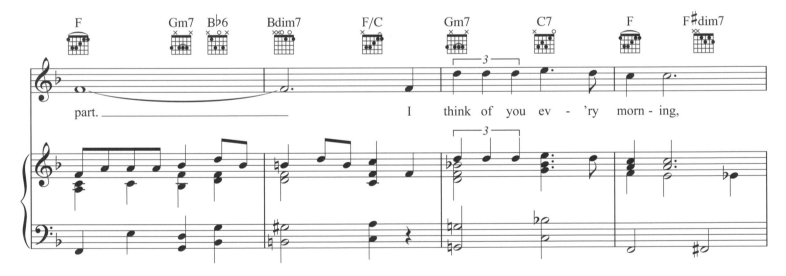

part. _____ I think of you ev-'ry morn-ing,

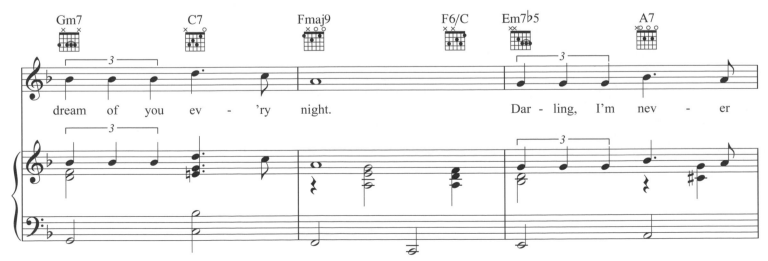

dream of you ev-'ry night. Dar-ling, I'm nev-er

lone - ly when - ev - er _____ you're in sight. I

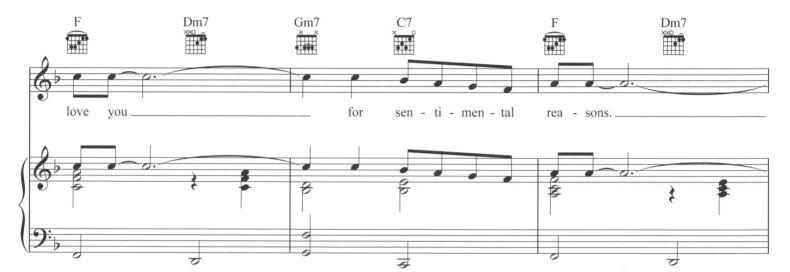

love you _____ for sen - ti - men - tal rea - sons. _____

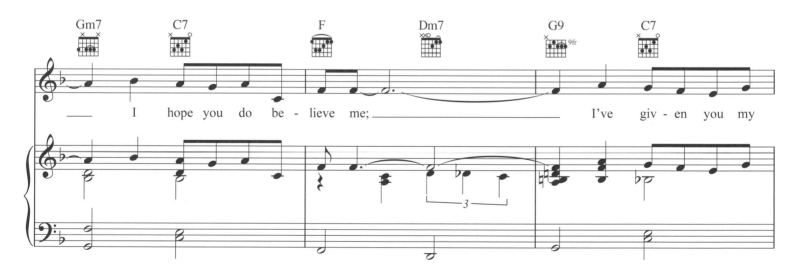

___ I hope you do be - lieve me; _____ I've giv - en you my

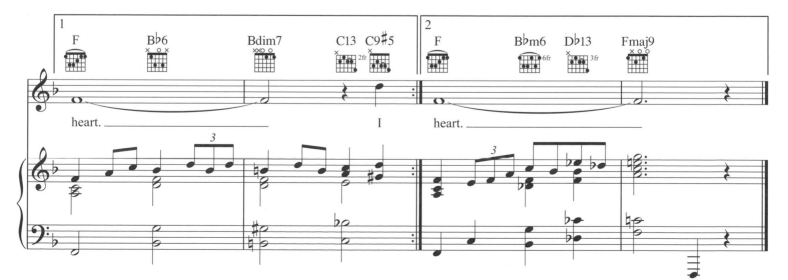

heart. _____ I heart. _____

DON'T GET AROUND MUCH ANYMORE

Words and Music by DUKE ELLINGTON
and BOB RUSSELL

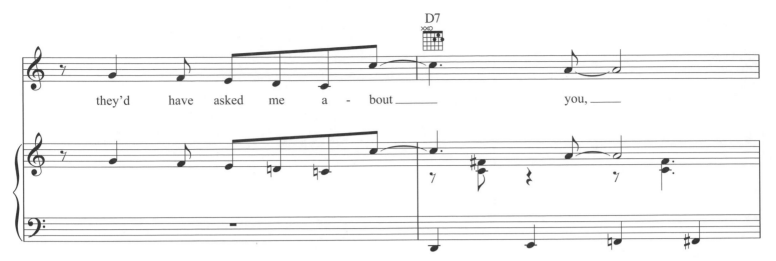

they'd have asked me a - bout _____ you, _____

don't get a - round much an - y - more. _____

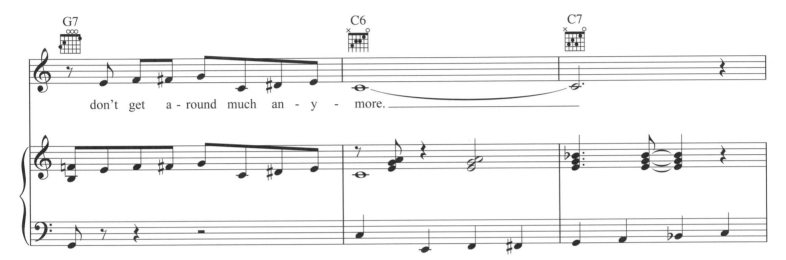

Dar - ling, I guess ___ my mind's more at ease, ___

___ but, nev - er - the - less, ___

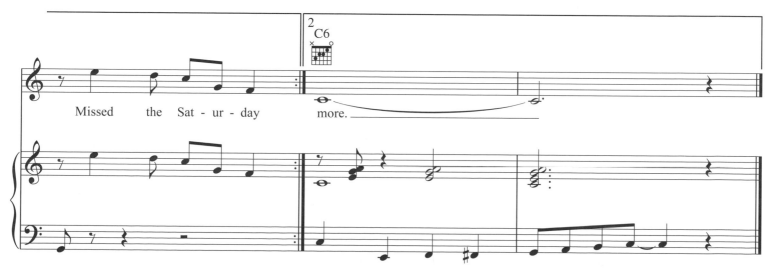

DON'T SIT UNDER THE APPLE TREE
(With Anyone Else but Me)

Words and Music by LEW BROWN,
SAM H. STEPT and CHARLIE TOBIAS

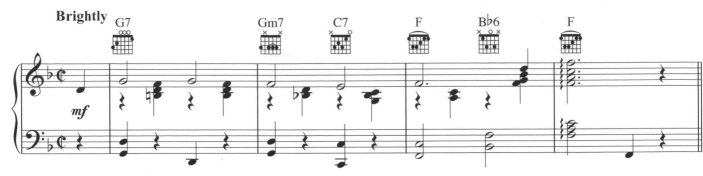

I wrote my moth-er, I wrote my fa-ther, and now I'm

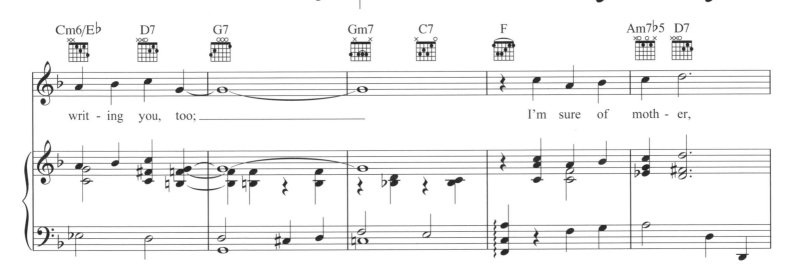

writ-ing you, too; _____ I'm sure of moth-er,

I'm sure of fa-ther, now I wan-na be sure of you. _____

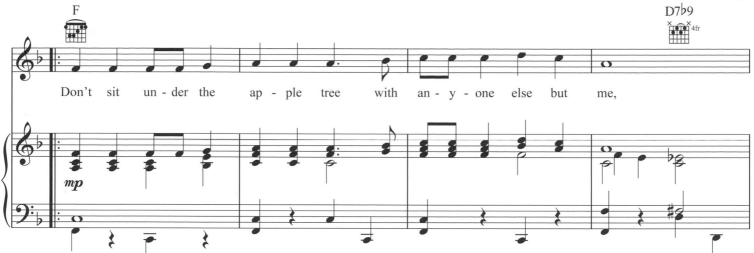

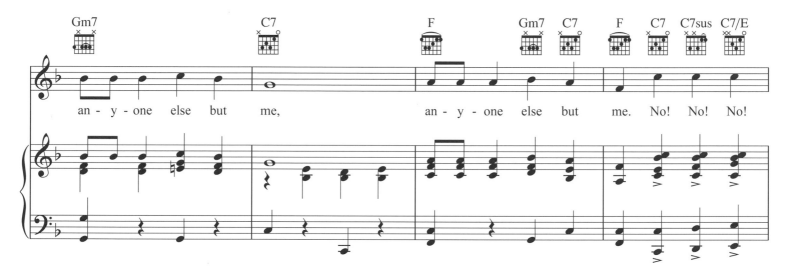

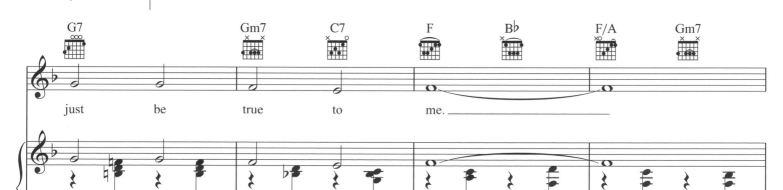

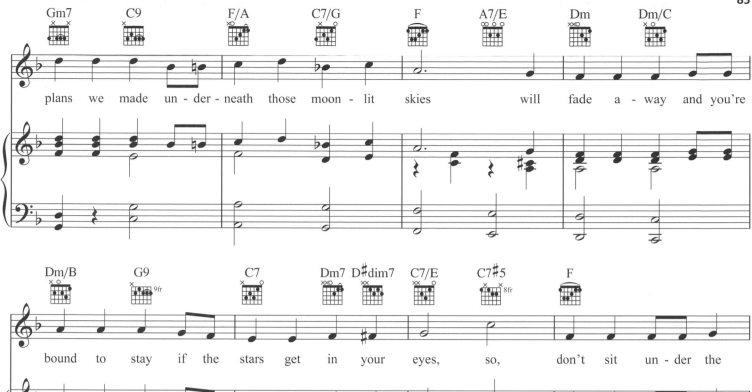

plans we made un - der - neath those moon - lit skies will fade a - way and you're

bound to stay if the stars get in your eyes, so, don't sit un - der the

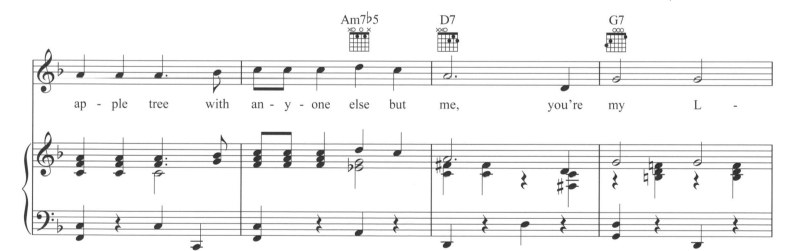

ap - ple tree with an - y - one else but me, you're my L -

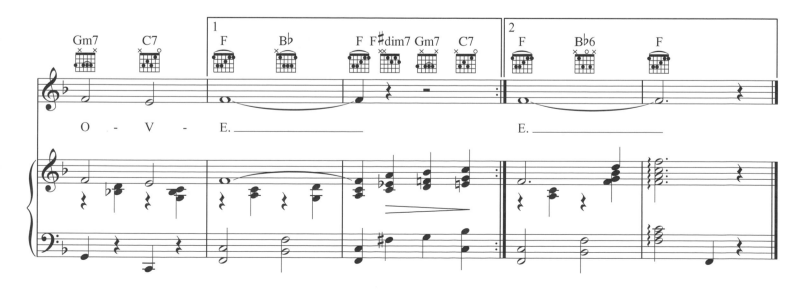

O - V - E. _____ E. _____

FIVE FOOT TWO, EYES OF BLUE
(Has Anybody Seen My Girl?)

Words by JOE YOUNG and SAM LEWIS
Music by RAY HENDERSON

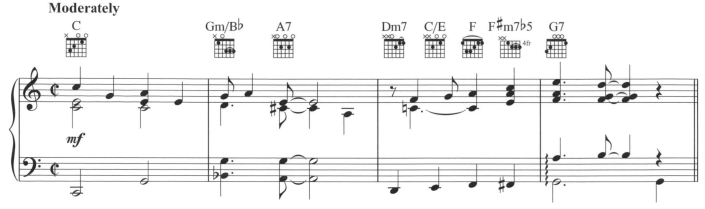

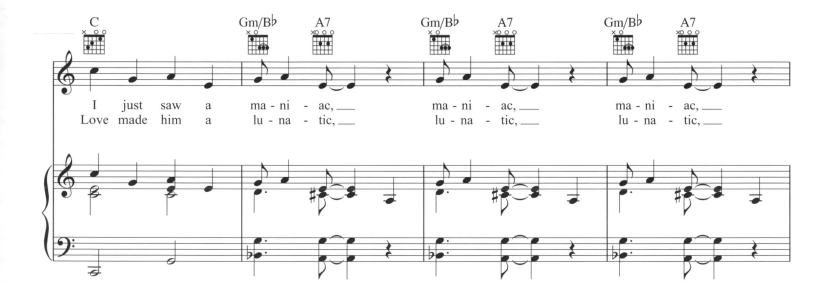

I just saw a ma - ni - ac, ___ ma - ni - ac, ___ ma - ni - ac, ___
Love made him a lu - na - tic, ___ lu - na - tic, ___ lu - na - tic, ___

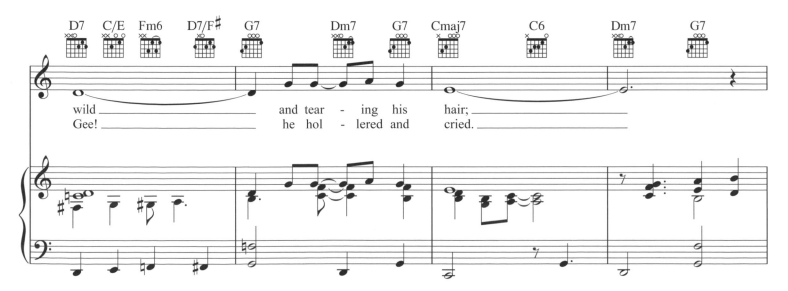

wild ___ and tear - ing his hair; ___
Gee! ___ he hol - lered and cried. ___

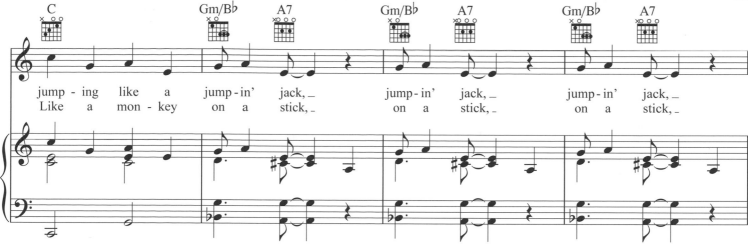

jump-ing like a jump-in' jack, ___ jump-in' jack, ___ jump-in' jack, ___
Like a mon-key on a stick, ___ on a stick, ___ on a stick, ___

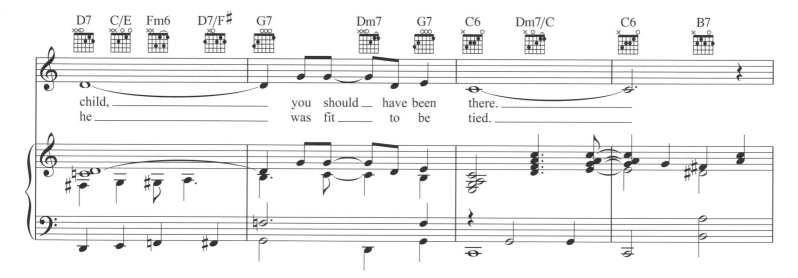

child, _____ you should ___ have been there. _____
he _____ was fit _____ to be tied. _____

Laughed so loud I thought that I would cave in,
When we asked him for his wife's de - scrip - tion,

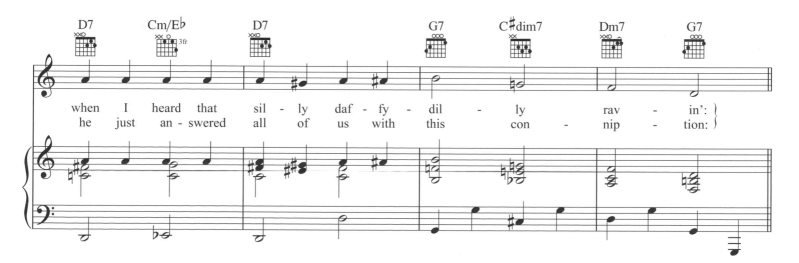

when I heard that sil - ly daf - fy - dil - ly rav - in': }
he just an - swered all of us with this con - nip - tion: }

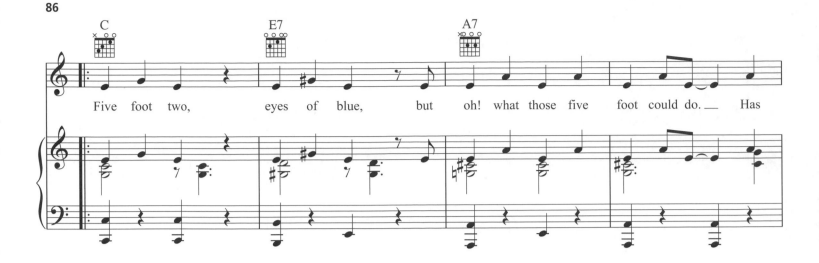

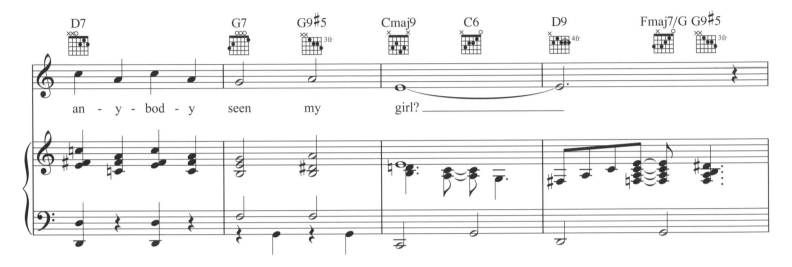

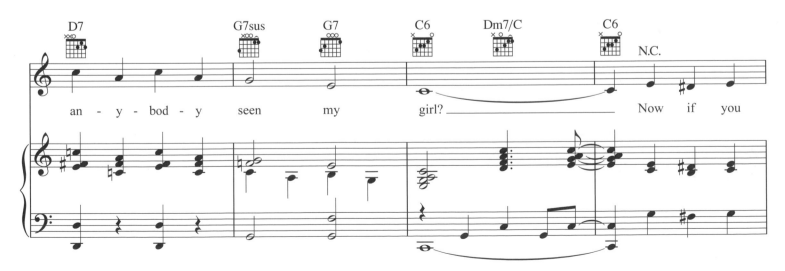

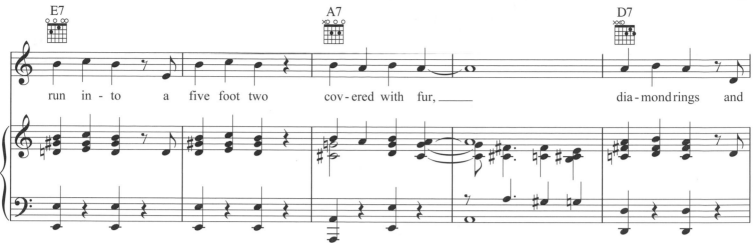

run in-to a five foot two cov-ered with fur, _____ dia-mond rings and

all those things, bet-cha' life it is-n't her. __ But could she love,

could she woo? Could she, could she, could she coo? __ Has an-y-bod-y seen my

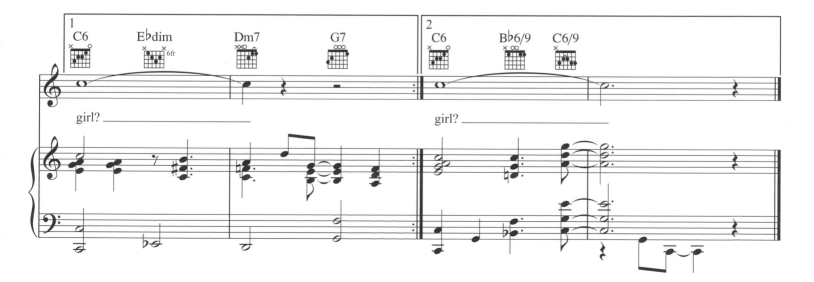

girl? _____ girl? _____

FLYING HOME

Music by BENNY GOODMAN
and LIONEL HAMPTON
Lyric by SID ROBIN

Moderate Bounce

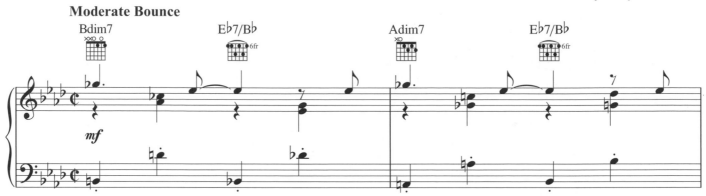

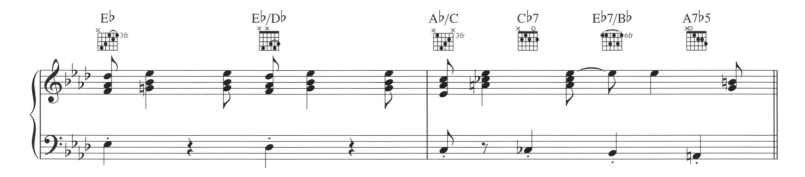

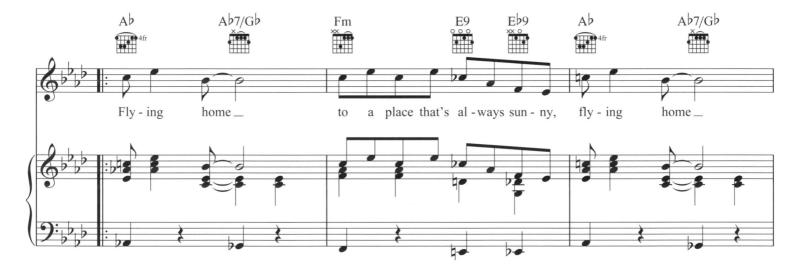

Fly-ing home __ to a place that's al-ways sun-ny, fly-ing home __

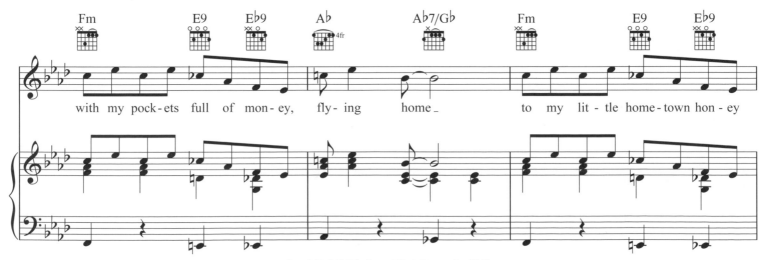

with my pock-ets full of mon-ey, fly-ing home __ to my lit-tle home-town hon-ey

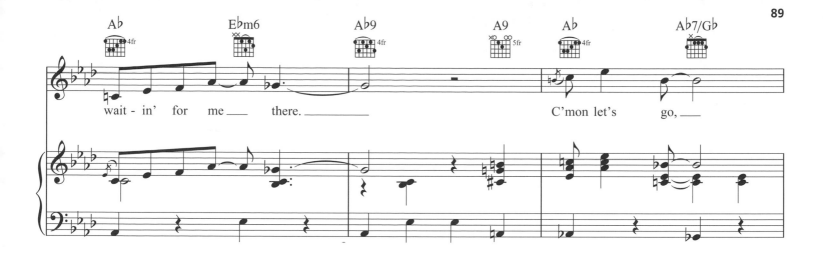

wait - in' for me ___ there. _____ C'mon let's go, ___

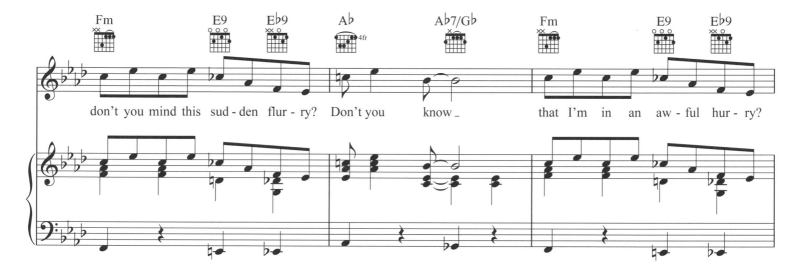

don't you mind this sud - den flur - ry? Don't you know _ that I'm in an aw - ful hur - ry?

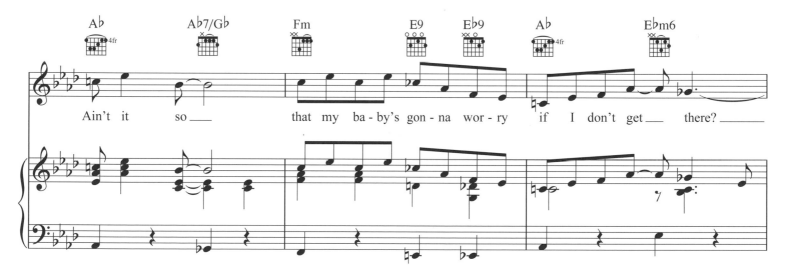

Ain't it so ___ that my ba - by's gon - na wor - ry if I don't get ___ there? _____

My ___ heart is burn - in' ev - er since I've been learn - in' how I

missed {her, / him,} since I kissed {her. / him.} Now —

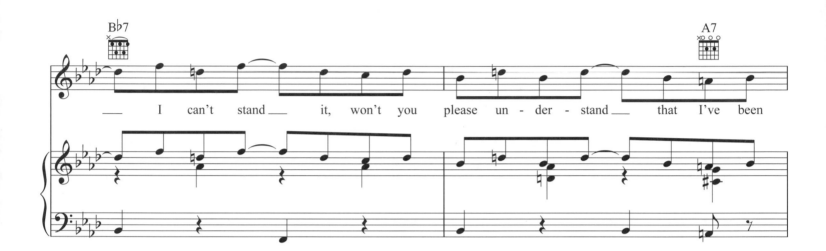

— I can't stand — it, won't you please un-der-stand — that I've been

lone-some, ———— I've been liv-ing by my own-some. Fly-ing home, —

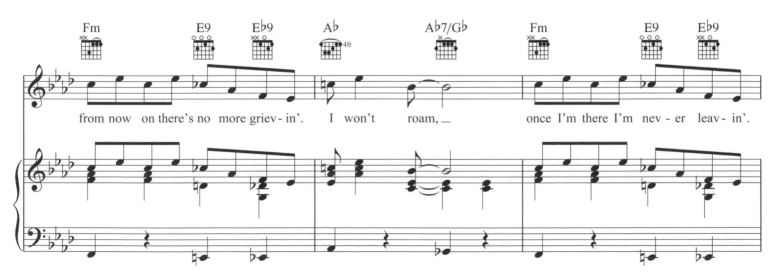

from now on there's no more griev-in'. I won't roam, — once I'm there I'm nev-er leav-in'.

Fly- ing home, ___ to that love I'll be re- ceiv- in'.

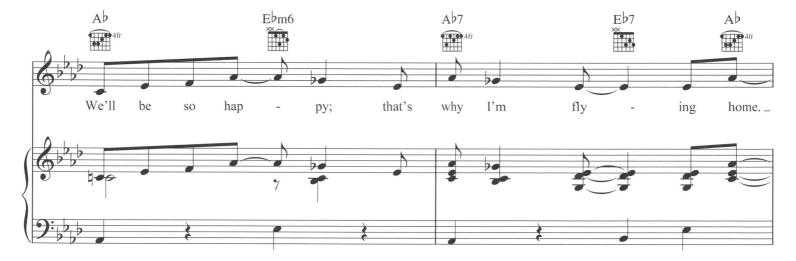

We'll be so hap- py; that's why I'm fly - ing home. __

FRENESÍ

Words and Music by
ALBERTO DOMÍNGUEZ

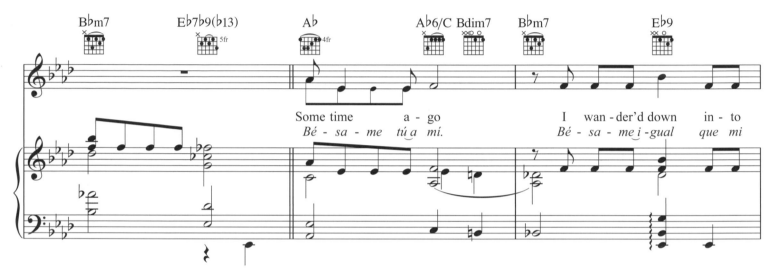

Some time a - go
Bé - sa - me tú a mí.

I wan - der'd down in - to
Bé - sa - me i - gual que mi

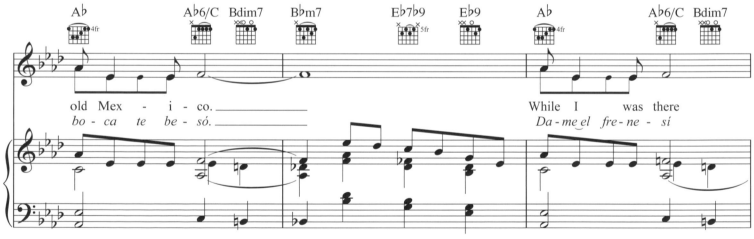

old Mex - i - co.
bo - ca te be - só.

While I was there
Da - me el fre - ne - sí

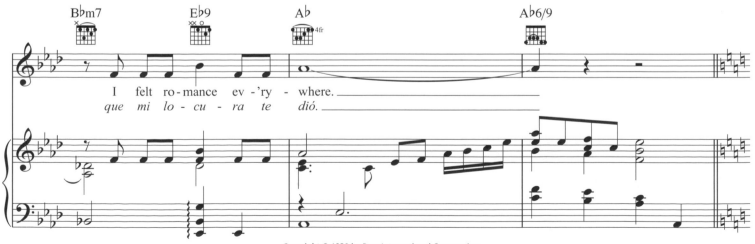

I felt ro - mance ev - 'ry - where.
que mi lo - cu - ra te dió.

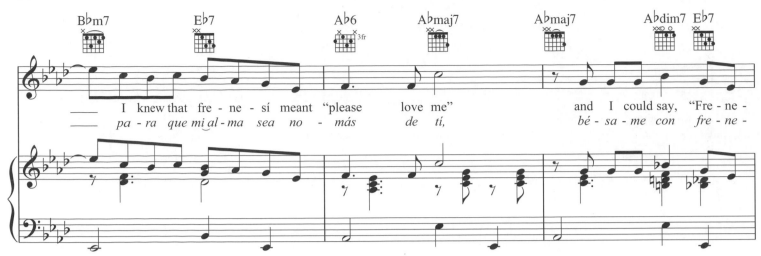

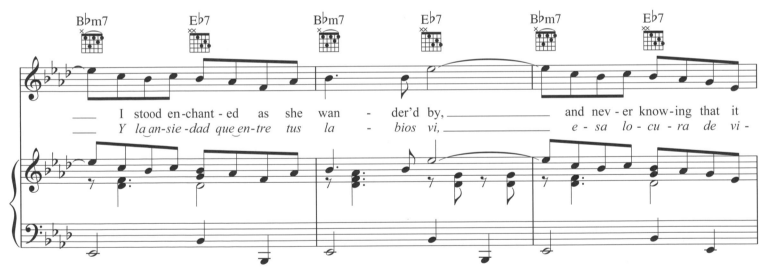

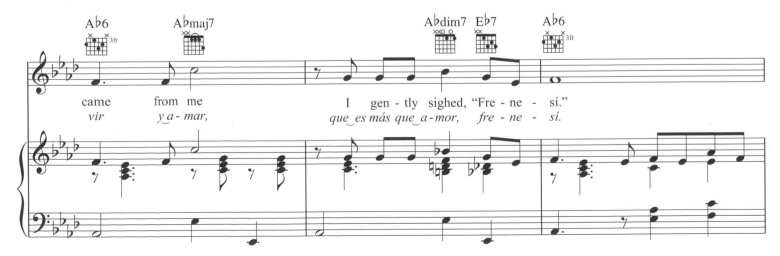

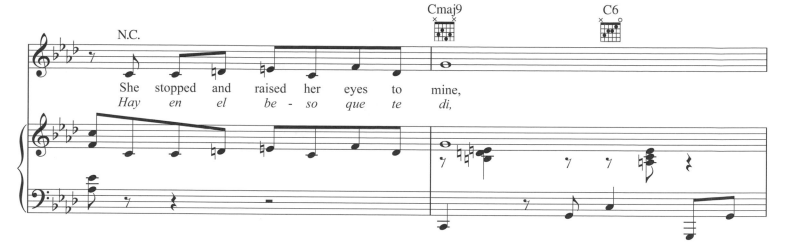

She stopped and raised her eyes to mine,
Hay en el be - so que te di,

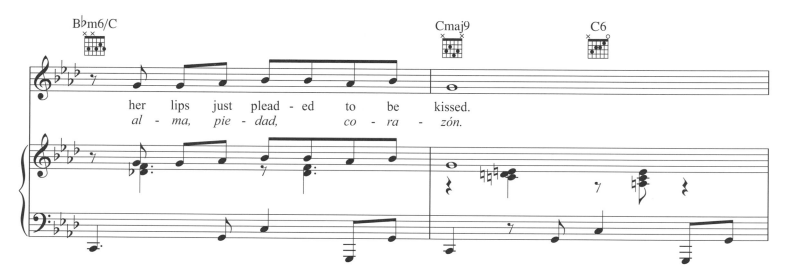

her lips just plead - ed to be kissed.
al - ma, pie - dad, co - ra - zón.

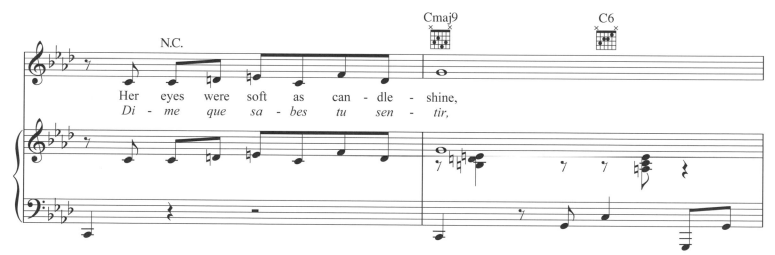

Her eyes were soft as can - dle - shine,
Di - me que sa - bes tu sen - tir,

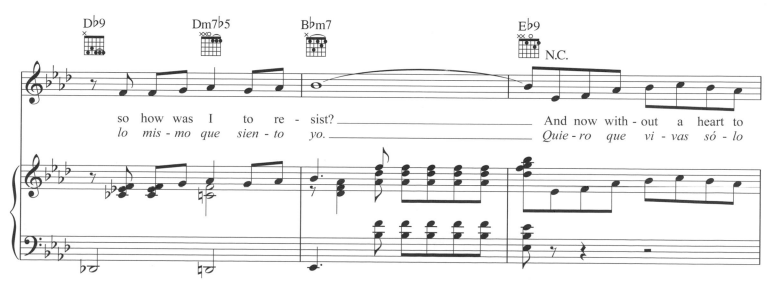

so how was I to re - sist? _____ And now with - out a heart to
lo mis - mo que sien - to yo._____ Quie - ro que vi - vas só - lo

call my own, _____ a great-er hap-pi-ness I've nev-er known _____
pa - ra mí _____ y que tú va - yas por don - de yo voy, _____

_____ be-cause her kiss-es are for me a-lone, who would-n't say, "Fre-ne-
_____ pa - ra que mi al - ma sea no - más de tí, bé - sa - me con fre - ne-

1
sí." It was Fi - es - ta down in sí." _____
sí. Quie - ro que vi - vas só - lo sí, _____

2

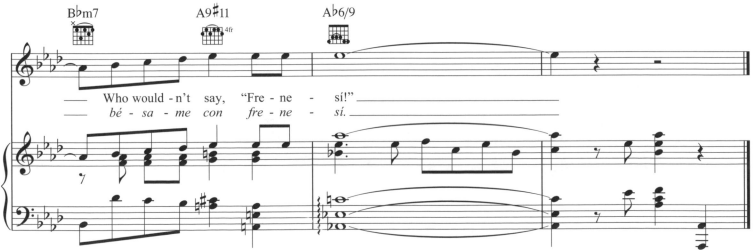

_____ Who would-n't say, "Fre - ne - sí!" _____
_____ bé - sa - me con fre - ne - sí. _____

HARLEM NOCTURNE

Words by EARLE HAGEN
Music by DICK ROGERS

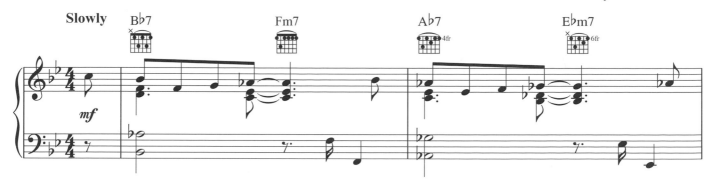

Deep mu-sic fills the night _____

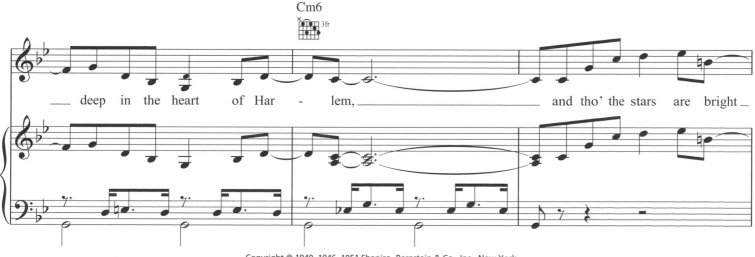

_____ deep in the heart of Har - lem, _____ and tho' the stars are bright _____

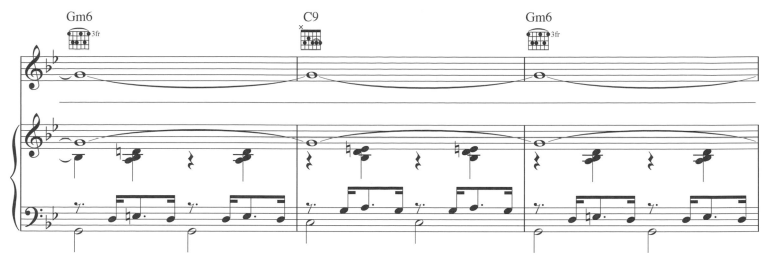

The mel-o-dy clings ___ a-round my heart strings, ___ it

won't let me go ___ when I'm lone-ly. ___ I

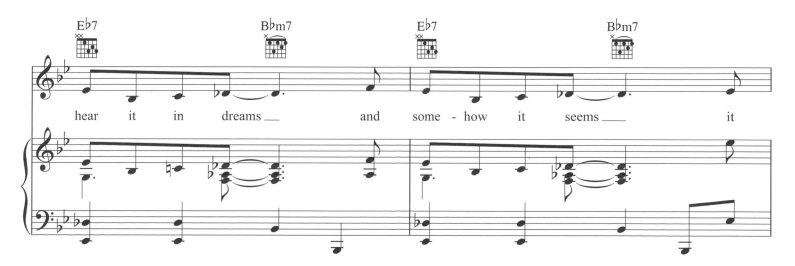

hear it in dreams ___ and some-how it seems ___ it

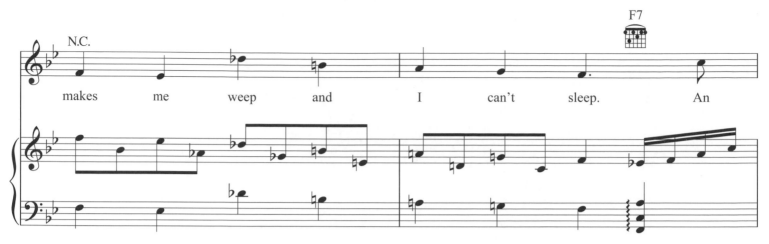

makes me weep and I can't sleep. An

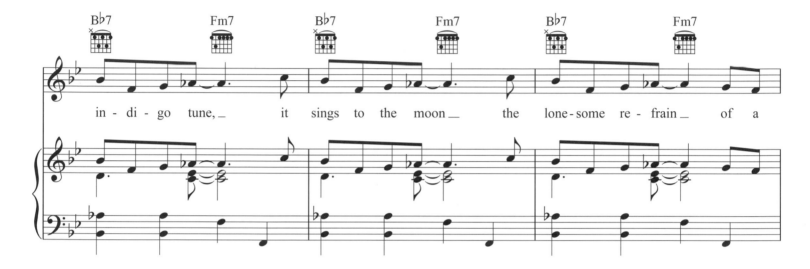

in - di - go tune, __ it sings to the moon __ the lone-some re-frain __ of a

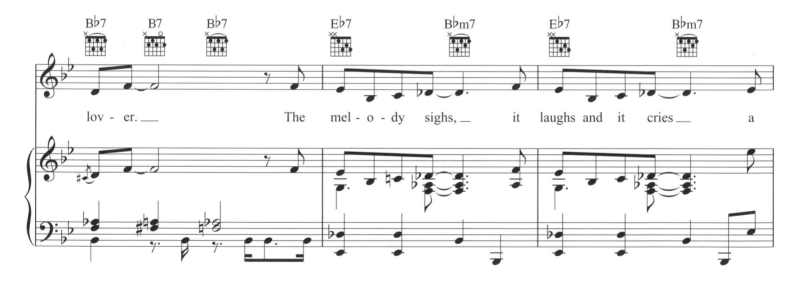

lov - er. ___ The mel - o - dy sighs, __ it laughs and it cries __ a

moan in blue that wails the long night

I CAN'T GET STARTED

from ZIEGFELD FOLLIES

Words by IRA GERSHWIN
Music by VERNON DUKE

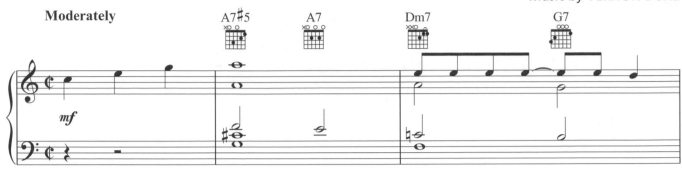

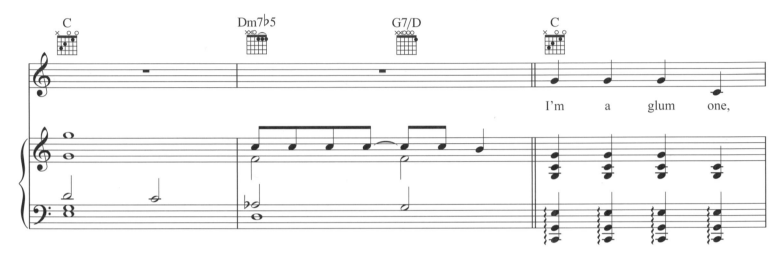

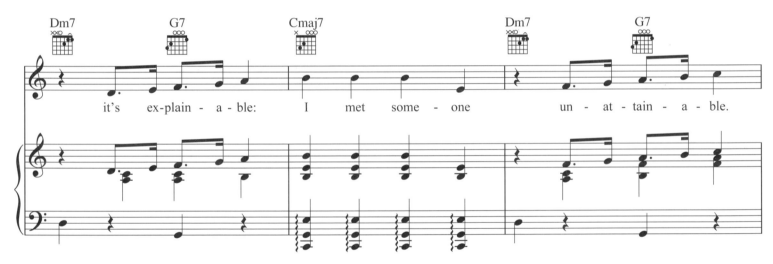

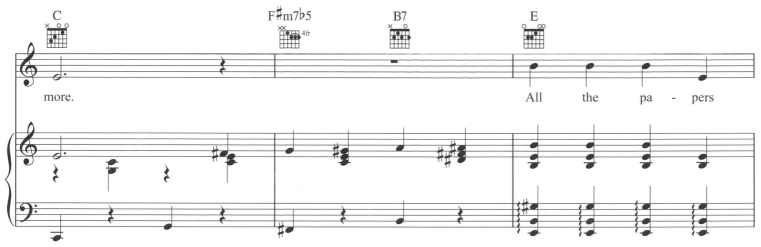

more.   All the pa - pers

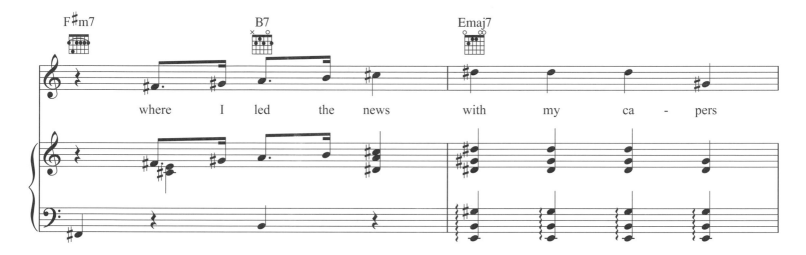

where I led the news with my ca - pers

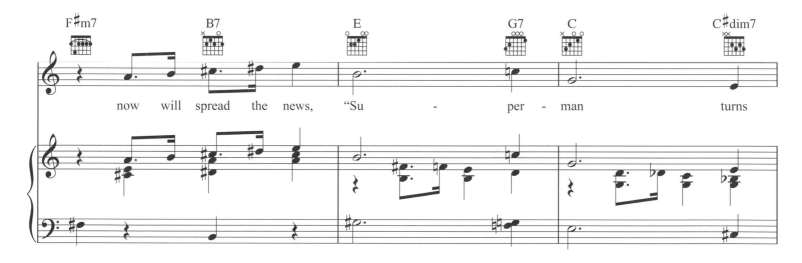

now will spread the news, "Su - per - man turns

out to be flash in the pan!" _____ I've flown a -

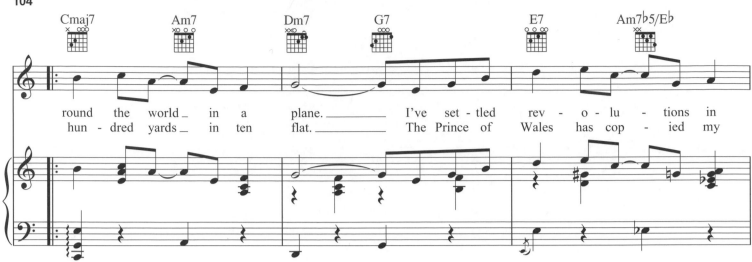

round the world___ in a plane._____ I've set-tled rev-o-lu-tions in
hun-dred yards___ in ten flat._____ The Prince of Wales has cop-ied my

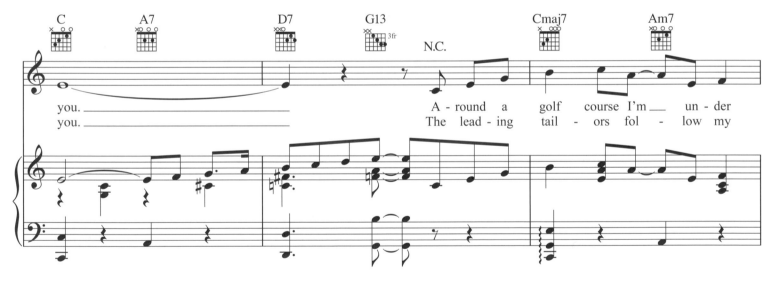

Spain._____ The North Pole I have chart-ed, but can't get start-ed with
hat._____ With queens I've à la cart-ed, but can't get start-ed with

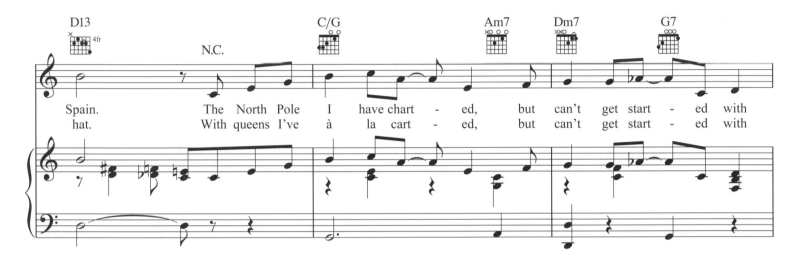

you._____ A-round a golf course I'm___ un-der
you._____ The lead-ing tail-ors fol-low my

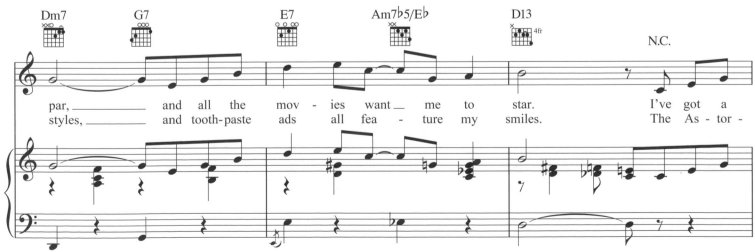

par,_____ and all the mov-ies want___ me to star._____ I've got a
styles,_____ and tooth-paste ads all fea-ture my smiles._____ The As-tor-

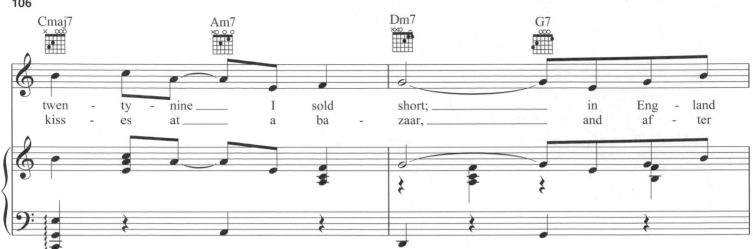

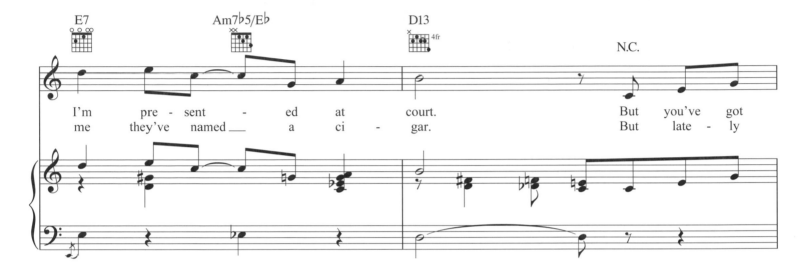

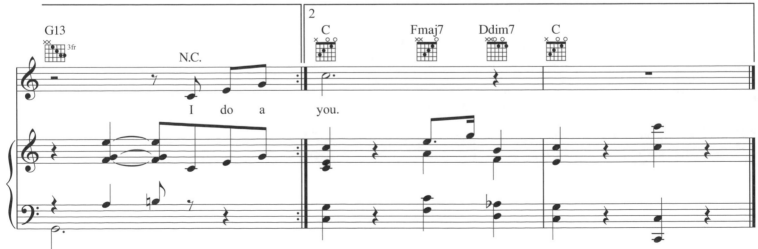

I'LL NEVER SMILE AGAIN

Words and Music by
RUTH LOWE

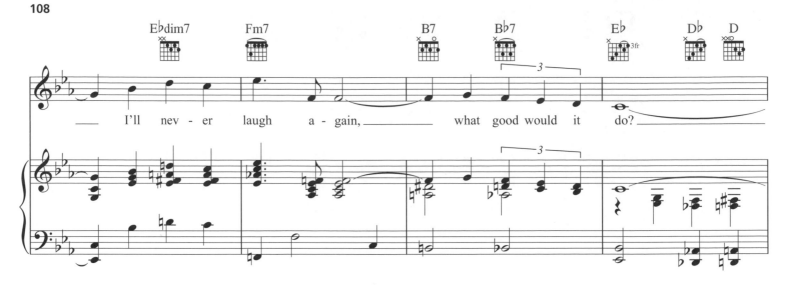

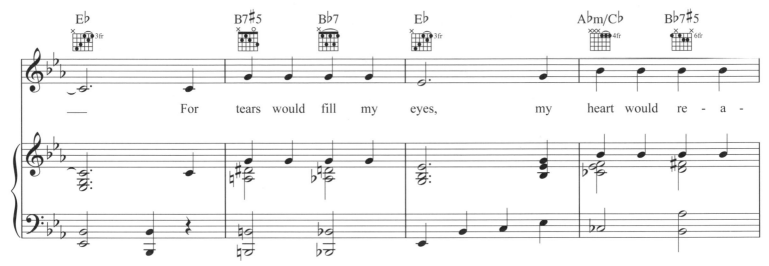

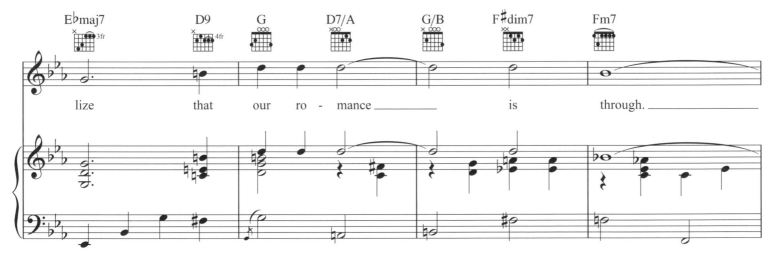

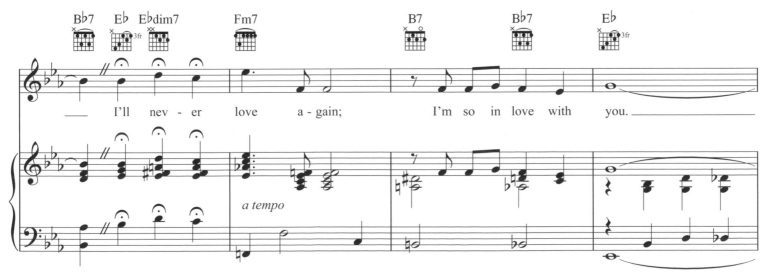

I'll nev-er thrill a-gain to some-bod-y

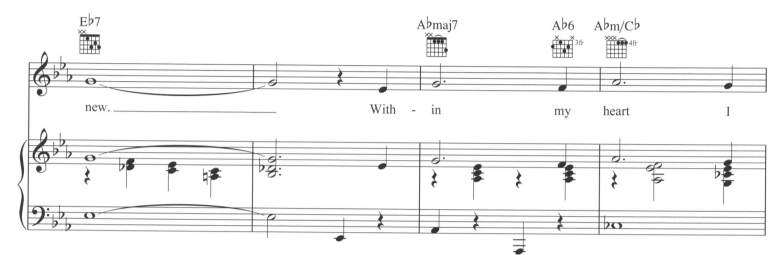

new. With-in my heart I

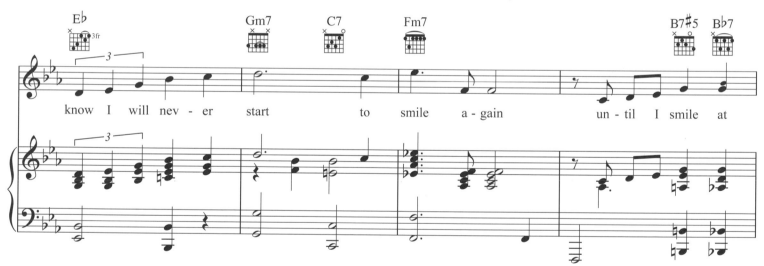

know I will nev-er start to smile a-gain un-til I smile at

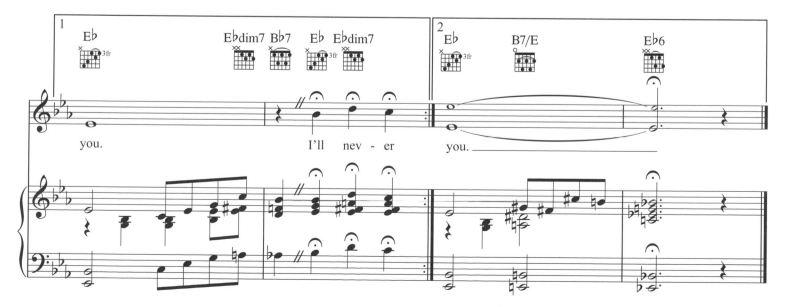

you. I'll nev-er you.

I CAN'T GIVE YOU ANYTHING BUT LOVE

from BLACKBIRDS OF 1928

Words and Music by JIMMY McHUGH
and DOROTHY FIELDS

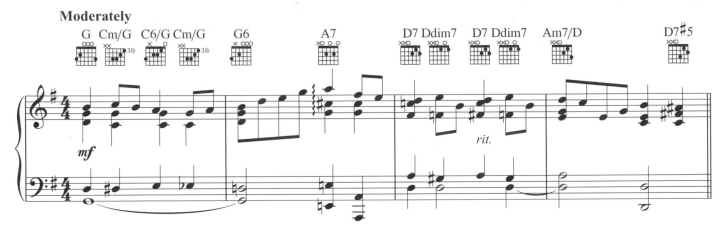

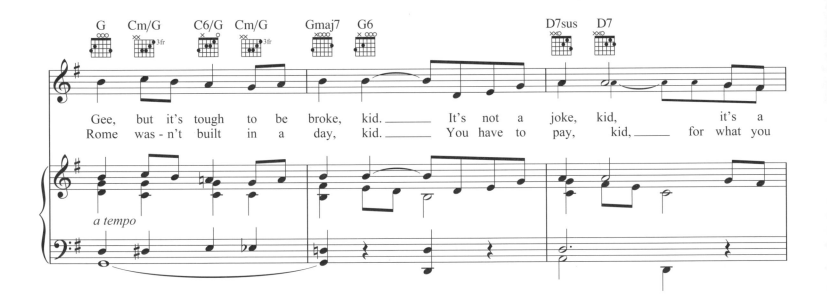

Gee, but it's tough to be broke, kid.____ It's not a joke, kid, it's a
Rome was-n't built in a day, kid.____ You have to pay, kid,____ for what you

curse.
get.

My luck is chang-ing, it's got-ten____ from sim-ply
But I am will-ing to wait, dear;____ your lit-tle

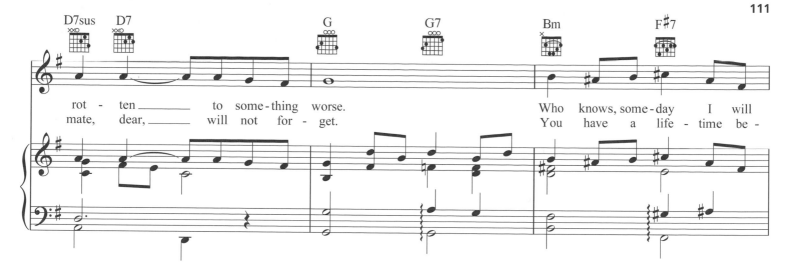

rot - ten _____ to some-thing worse. Who knows, some-day I will
mate, dear, _____ will not for-get. You have a life-time be-

win, too. I'll be - gin to reach my prime.
fore you. I'll a - dore you, come what may.

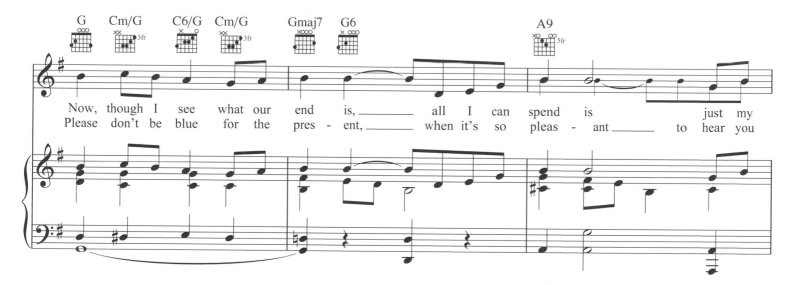

Now, though I see what our end is, _____ all I can spend is just my
Please don't be blue for the pres - ent, _____ when it's so pleas - ant _____ to hear you

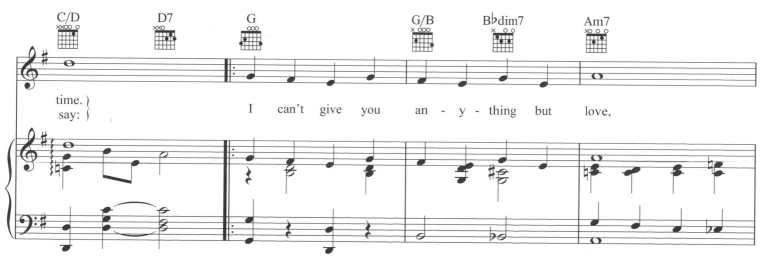

time. }
say: } I can't give you an - y - thing but love,

ba - by. That's the on - ly thing I've plen - ty of,

ba - by. Dream a - while, scheme a - while; we're sure to find __

__ hap - pi - ness and I guess all those things you've

al - ways pined for. Gee, I'd like to see you look - ing

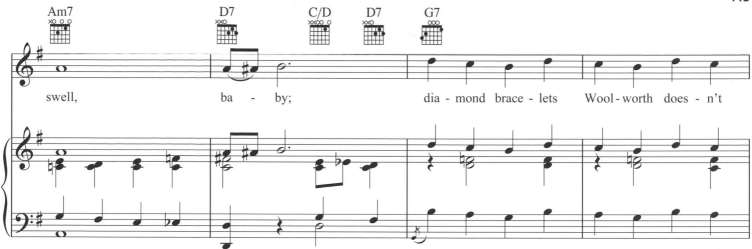

swell,	ba - by;	dia - mond brace - lets Wool - worth does - n't

sell,	ba - by.	Till that luck - y day, you know darned

well,	ba - by,	I can't give you an - y - thing but

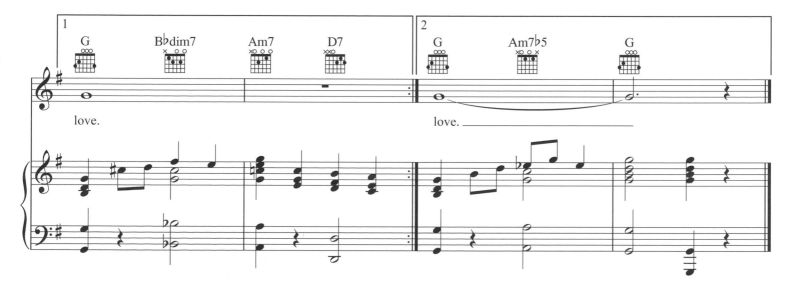

love.	love. _____

I'LL REMEMBER APRIL

Words and Music by PAT JOHNSTON,
DON RAYE and GENE DePAUL

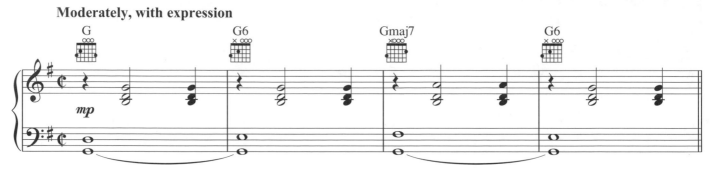

Moderately, with expression

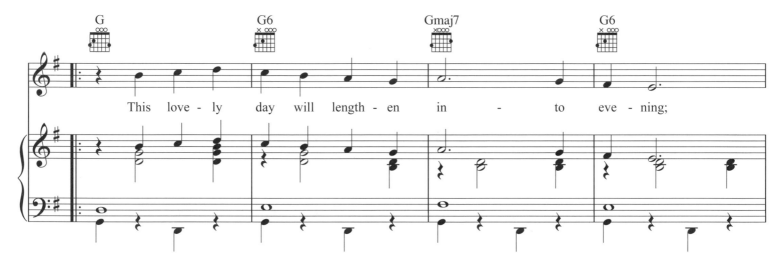

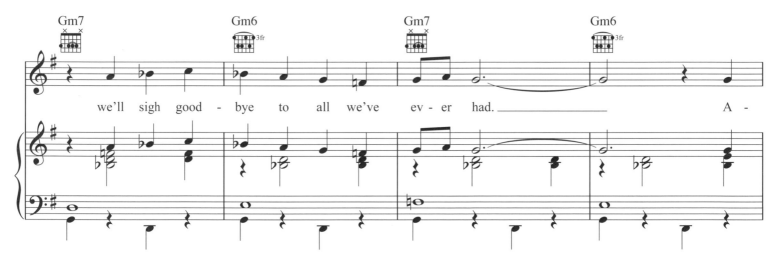

This love-ly day will length-en in - to eve-ning;

we'll sigh good-bye to all we've ev-er had. _____ A -

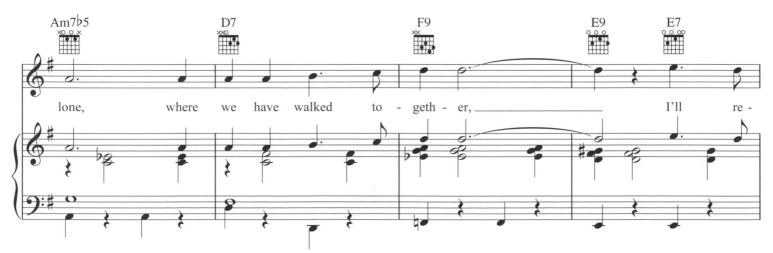

lone, where we have walked to-geth-er, _____ I'll re-

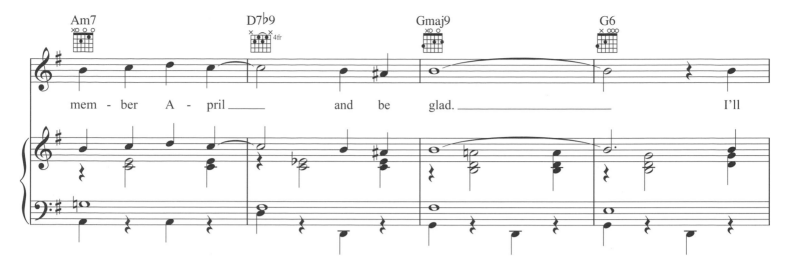

- mem - ber A - pril ____ and be glad. _____ I'll

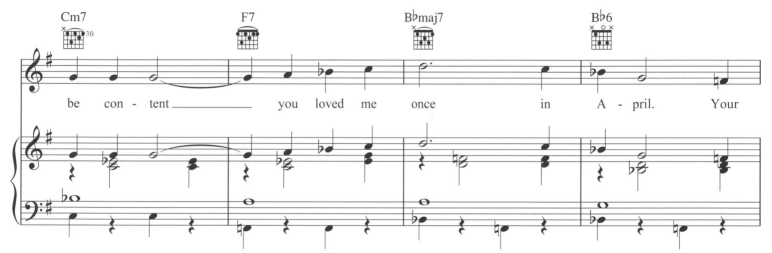

be con - tent _____ you loved me once in A - pril. Your

lips were warm _____ and love and spring were new. _____

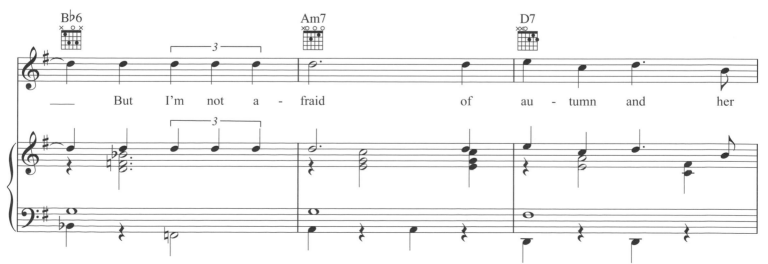

____ But I'm not a - fraid of au - tumn and her

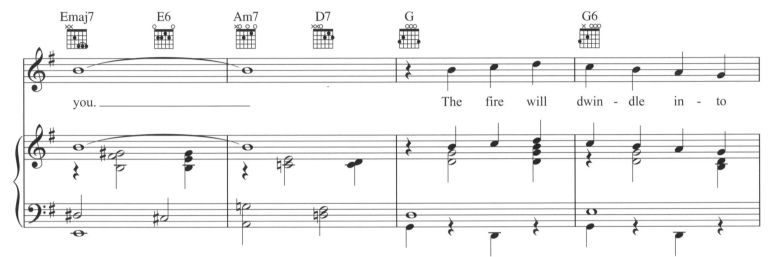

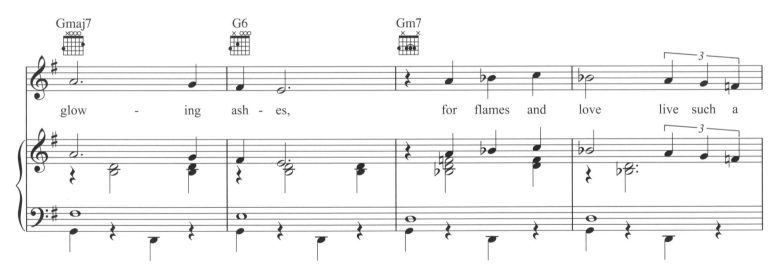

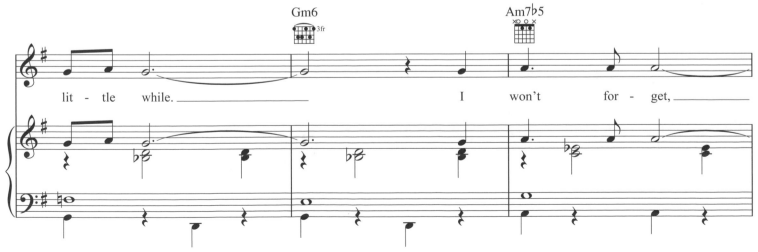

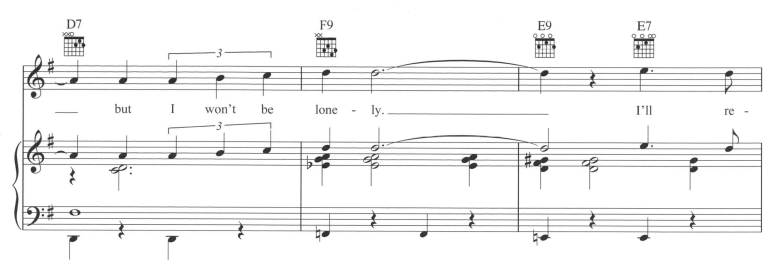

but I won't be lone - ly. _____ I'll re -

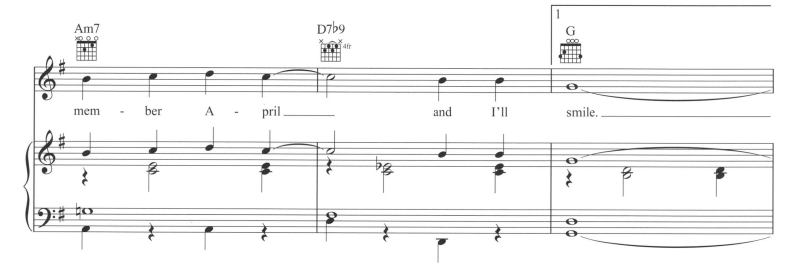

mem - ber A - pril ____ and I'll smile. ____

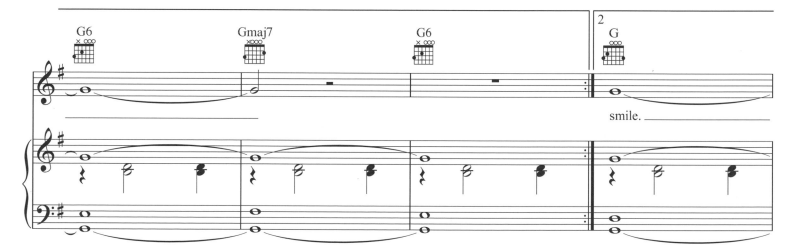

smile.

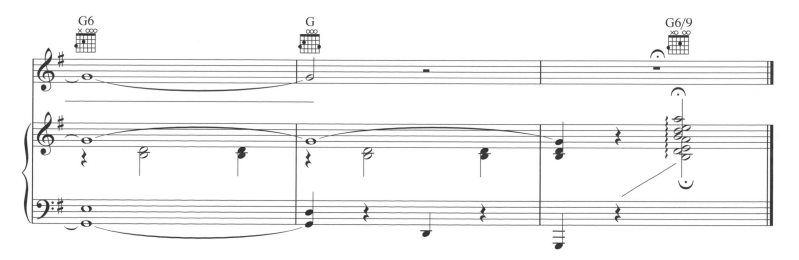

IN THE MOOD

By JOE GARLAND

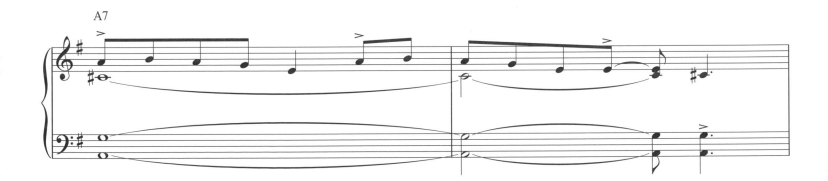

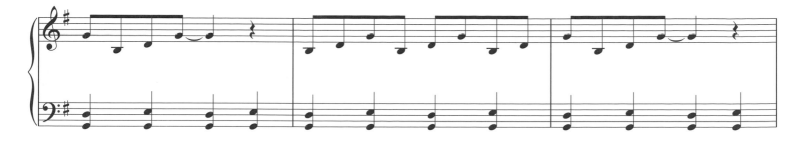

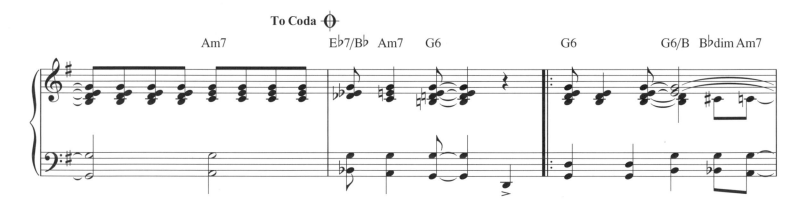

IT'S A PITY TO SAY GOODNIGHT

Words and Music by
BILLY REID

Moderately, with a relaxed beat

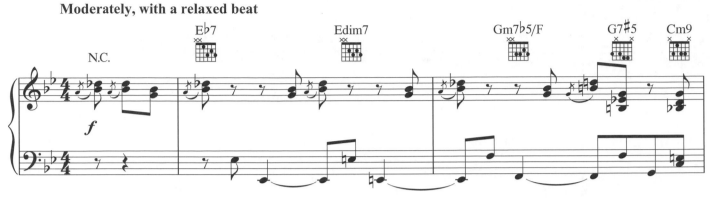

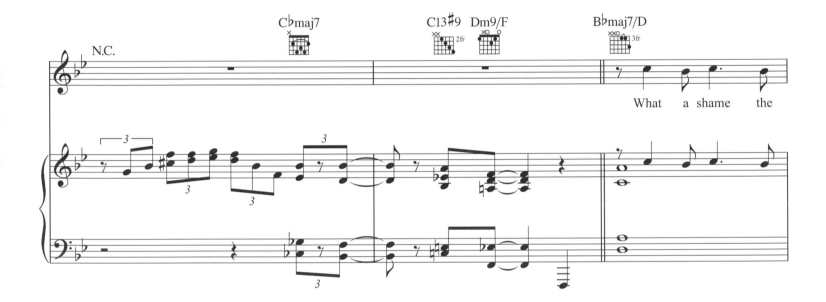

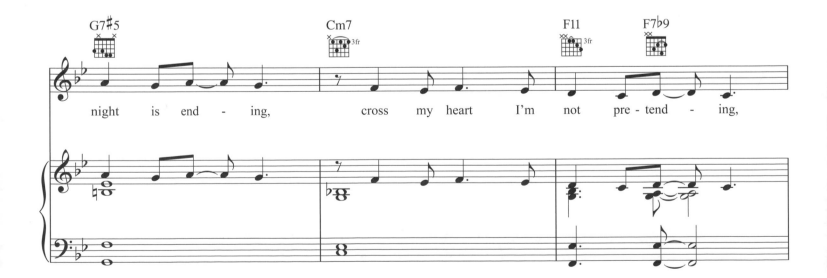

What a shame the night is end - ing, cross my heart I'm not pre - tend - ing,

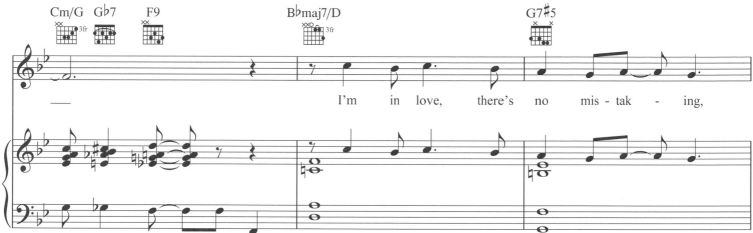

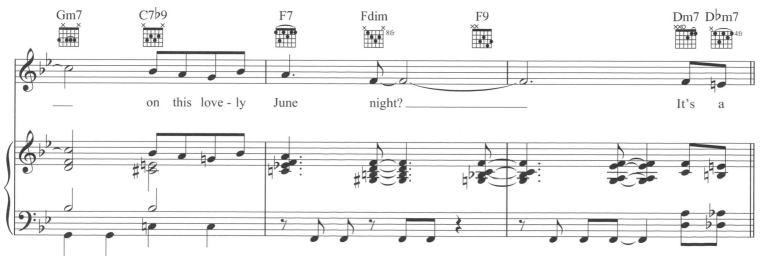

pit - y to say ____ "good - night," _____ be - cause I

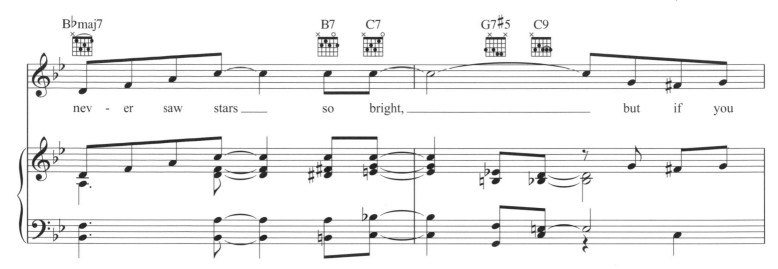

nev - er saw stars ____ so bright, _____ but if you

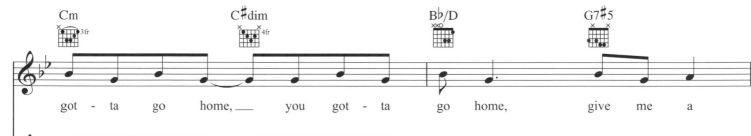

got - ta go home, ___ you got - ta go home, give me a

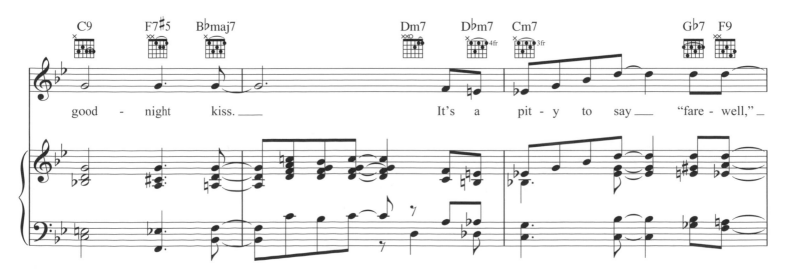

good - night kiss. ___ It's a pit - y to say ____ "fare - well," __

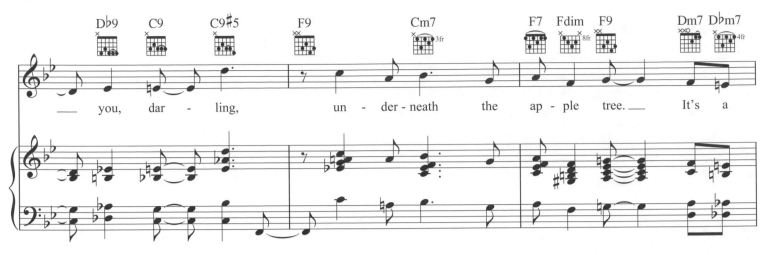

_____ you, dar - ling, un - der - neath the ap - ple tree. ____ It's a

pit - y to say ____ "good - night," _____ be - cause I want you to hold ____ me tight, ____

_____ but if you got - ta go home, ____ you got - ta go home, give me a

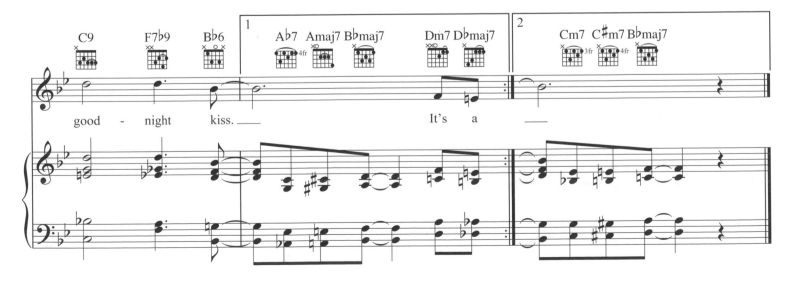

good - night kiss. ____ It's a ____

LAZY RIVER

from THE BEST YEARS OF OUR LIVES

Words and Music by HOAGY CARMICHAEL
and SIDNEY ARODIN

I like la - zy weath - er, I like la - zy days;

can't be blamed for hav - ing la - zy ways. Some old la - zy riv - er

sleeps be - side my door, whis - p'ring to the sun - lit shore.

JUMPIN' AT THE WOODSIDE

Music by COUNT BASIE
Words by JON HENDRICKS

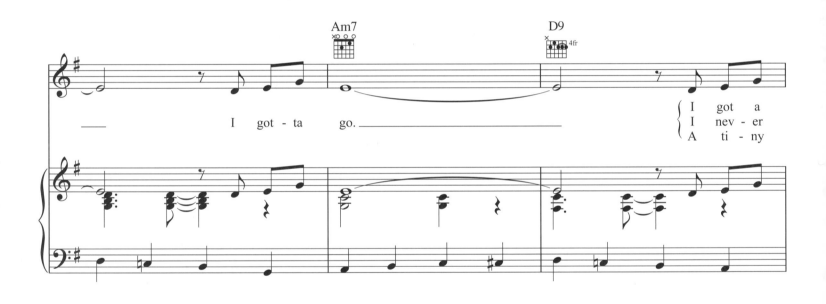

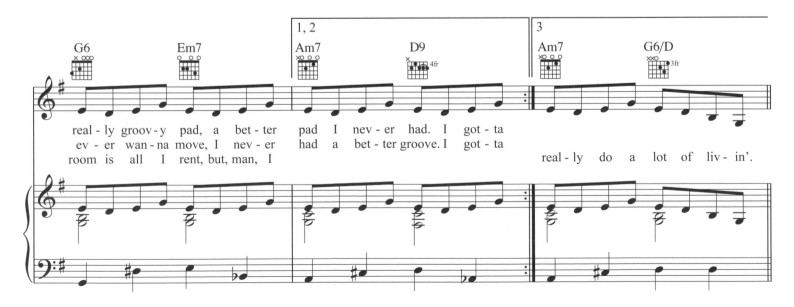

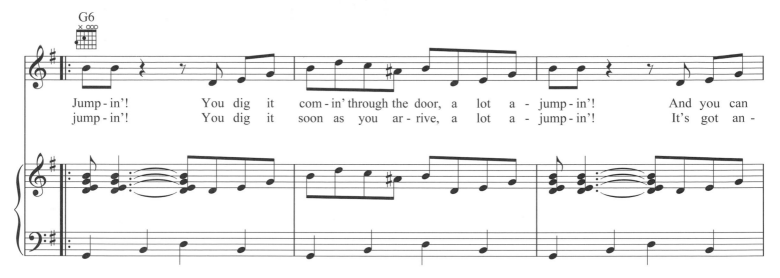

Jump - in'! You dig it com - in' through the door, a lot a - jump - in'! And you can

jump - in'! You dig it soon as you ar - rive, a lot a - jump - in'! It's got an -

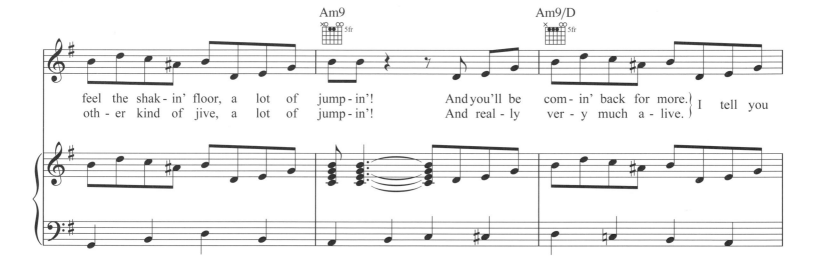

feel the shak - in' floor, a lot of jump - in'! And you'll be com - in' back for more. I tell you

oth - er kind of jive, a lot of jump - in'! And real - ly ver - y much a - live. I tell you

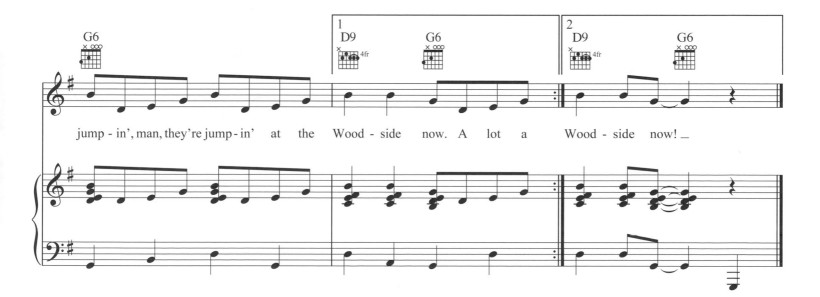

jump - in', man, they're jump - in' at the Wood - side now. A lot a Wood - side now! __

LEAP FROG

Words by LEO CORDAY
Music by JOE GARLAND

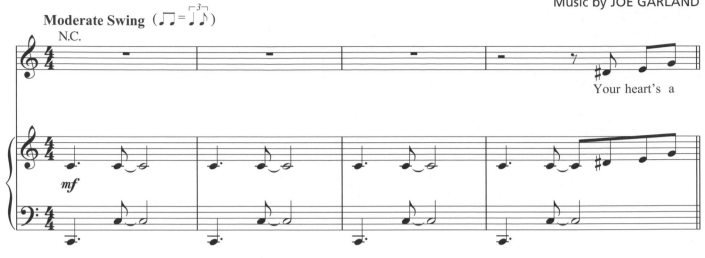

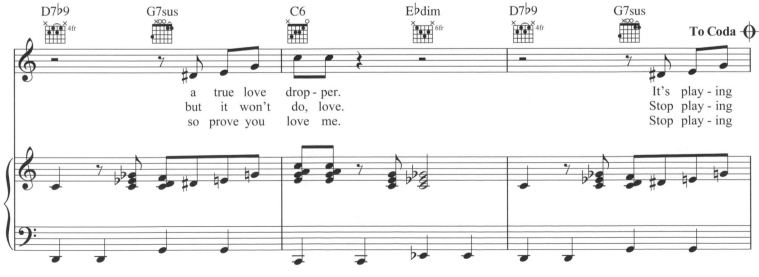

leap frog. __
leap frog. __

Each day a

You just

leap and look for brand-new charms. __ If you must jump, jump

in my arms. __ You hold __ me tight __ then hop __ from sight __ and that __

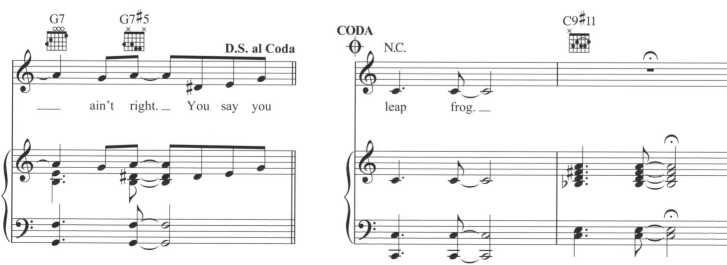

__ ain't right. __ You say you

leap frog. __

LET THERE BE LOVE

Lyric by IAN GRANT
Music by LIONEL RAND

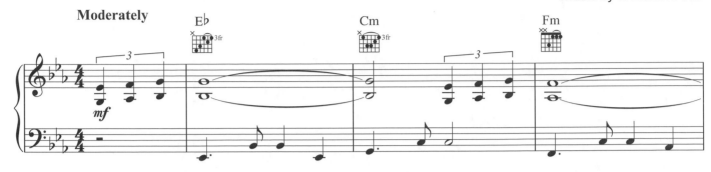

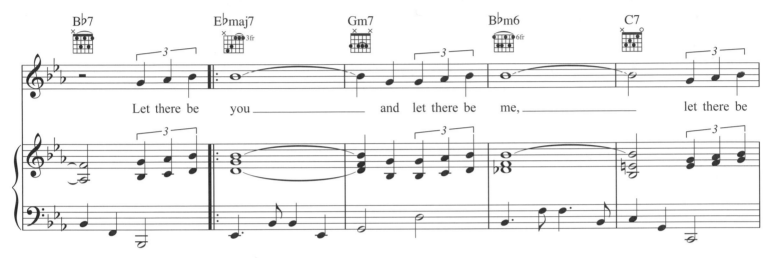

Let there be you _____ and let there be me, _____ let there be

oy - sters _____ un - der the sea. _____ Let there be wind, _____

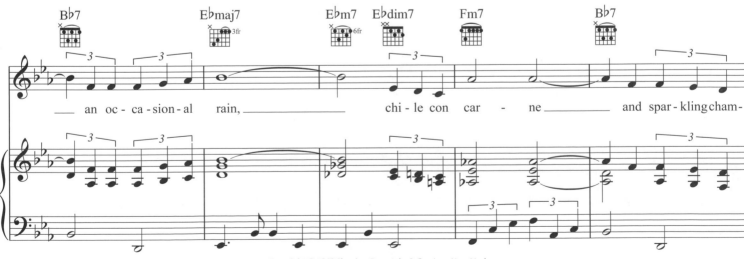

___ an oc - ca - sion - al rain, _____ chi - le con car - ne _____ and spar - kling cham-

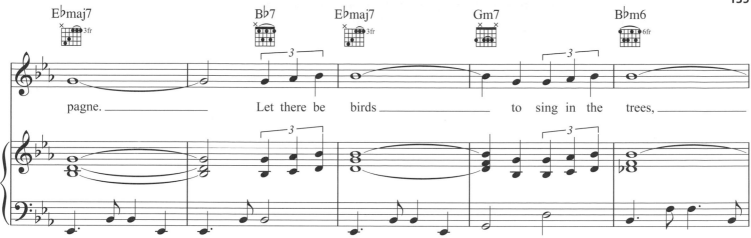

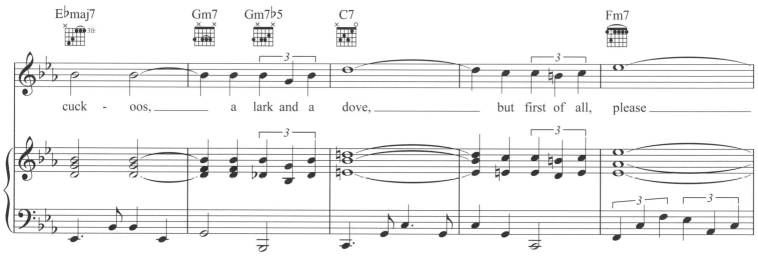

LET'S GET AWAY FROM IT ALL

Words and Music by TOM ADAIR
and MATT DENNIS

Let's take a trip___ in a trail - er, _____ no need to come_ back at all, __

___ let's take a pow - der to Bos - ton for chow - der,

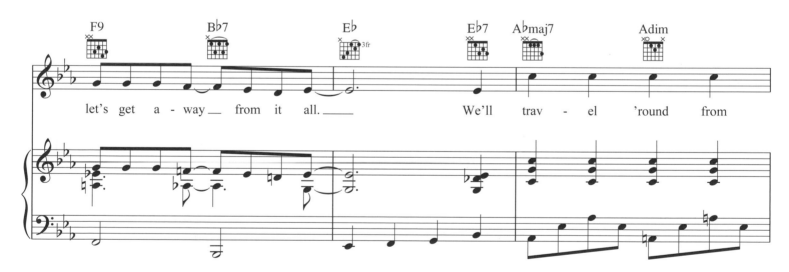

let's get a - way__ from it all. ___ We'll trav - el 'round from

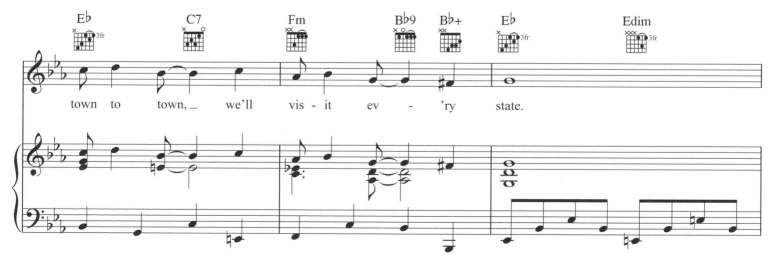

town to town,_ we'll vis - it ev - 'ry state.

I'll re - peat, "I love you, sweet!" ___ in all the for - ty - eight. ___

___ Let's go a - gain ___ to Ni - a - g'ra, ___

this time we'll look ___ at the "Fall," ___ let's leave our hut, ___ dear, get

out of our rut, ___ dear, let's get a - way ___ from it all. ___

MAIRZY DOATS

Words and Music by MILTON DRAKE,
AL HOFFMAN and JERRY LIVINGSTON

I know a dit-ty nut-ty as a fruit-cake,

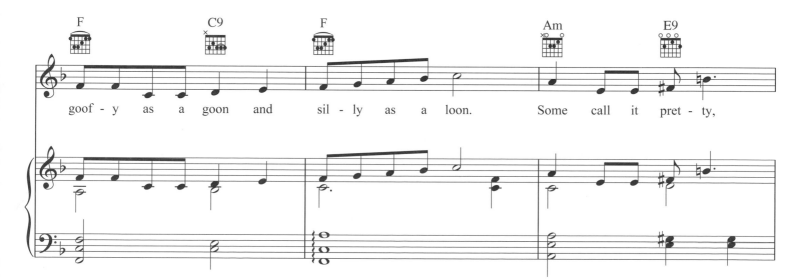

goof-y as a goon and sil-ly as a loon. Some call it pret-ty,

fun - ny to your ear, a lit - tle bit jum - bled and jiv - ey, sing,

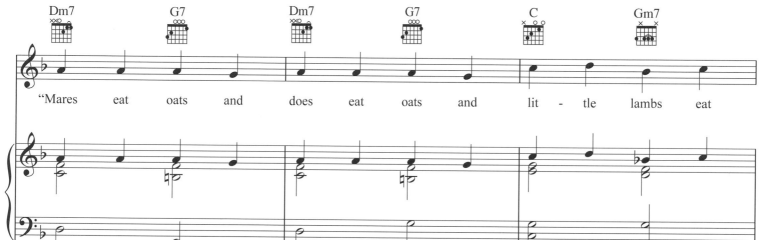

"Mares eat oats and does eat oats and lit - tle lambs eat

i - vy." Oh! Mair - zy doats and do - zy doats and lid - dle lam - zy div - ey; a

kid - dle - y div - ey too, would - n't you? _____ A kid - dle - y div - ey too, would - n't you?

MARIE

from the Motion Picture THE AWAKENING

Words and Music by
IRVING BERLIN

Moderate Swing tempo

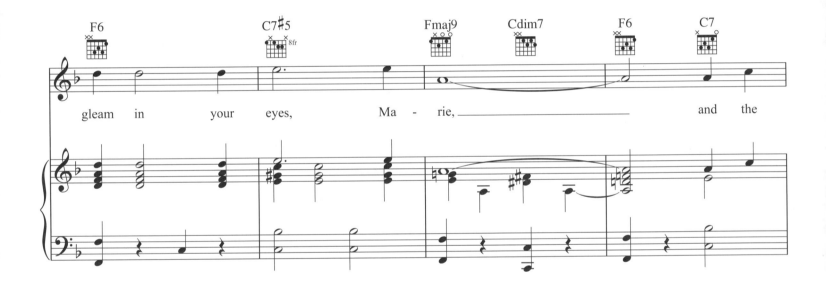

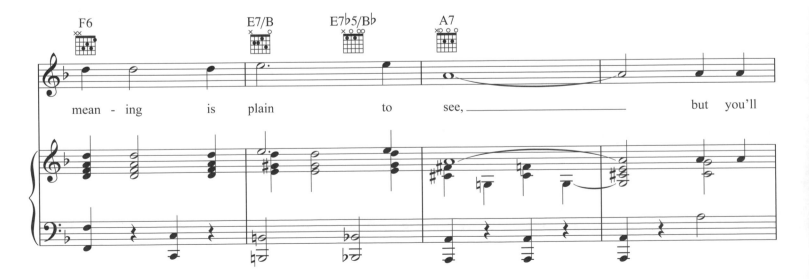

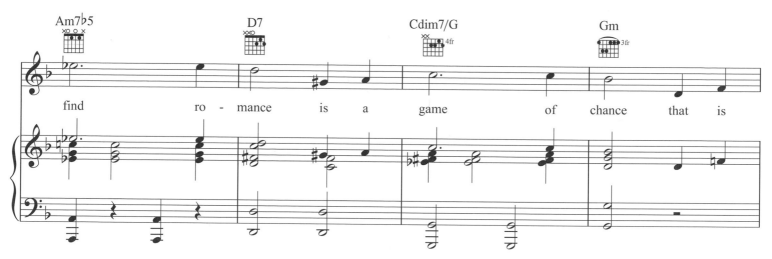

find ro - mance is a game of chance that is

not all it seems to be. _____ Ma -

rie, _____ the dawn is break - ing. Ma -

rie, _____ you'll soon be wak -

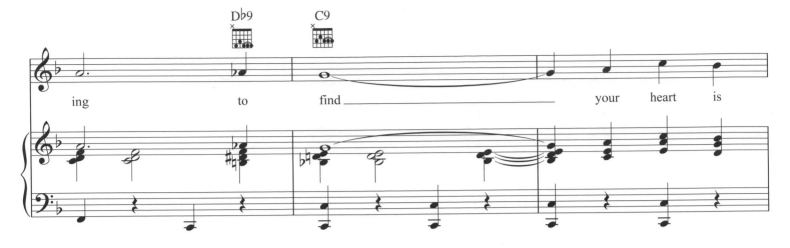

ing to find _____ your heart is

ach - ing and tears will fall as

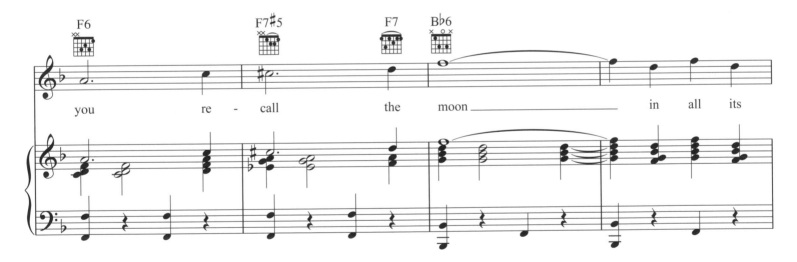

you re - call the moon _____ in all its

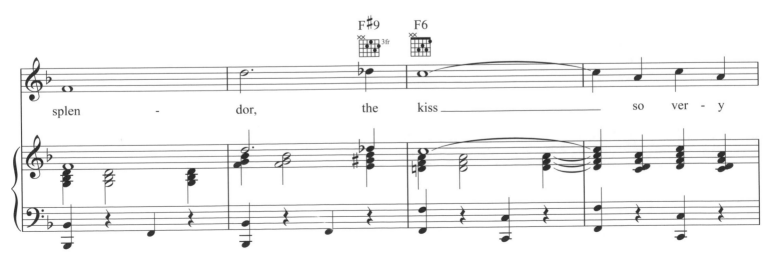

splen - dor, the kiss _____ so ver - y

ten - der, the words

"Will you sur - ren - der to

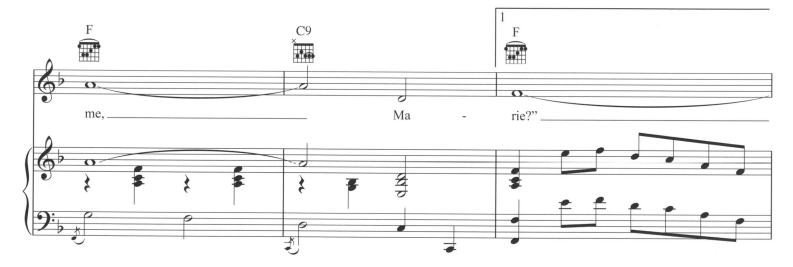

me, Ma - rie?"

1.

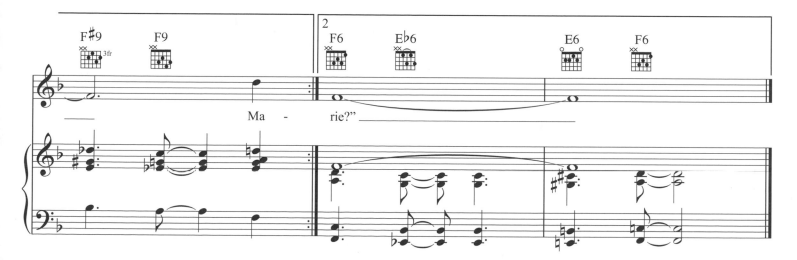

Ma - rie?"

MOOD INDIGO

Words and Music by DUKE ELLINGTON,
IRVING MILLS and ALBANY BIGARD

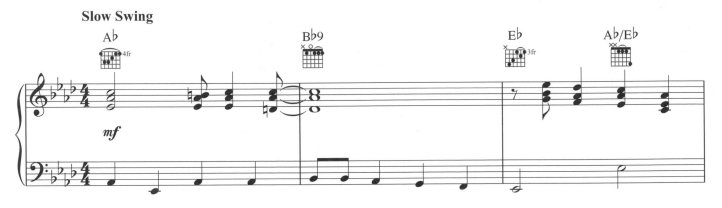

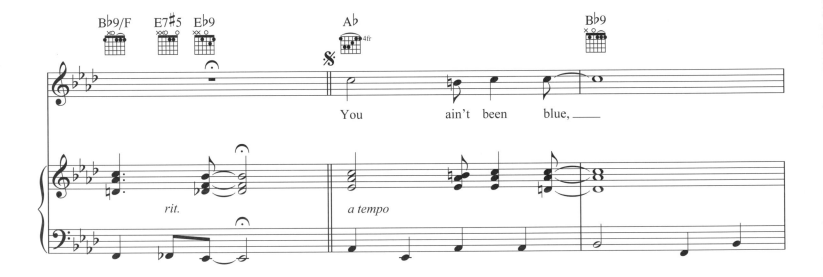

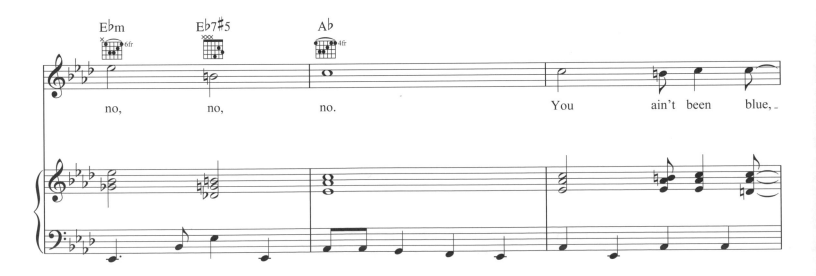

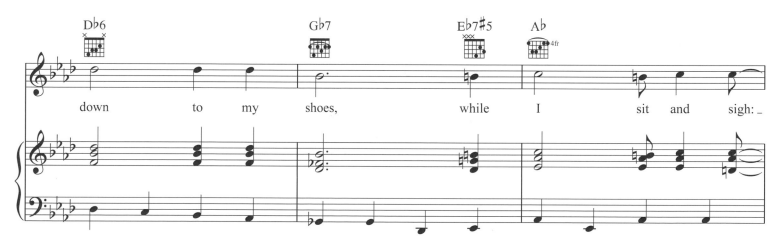

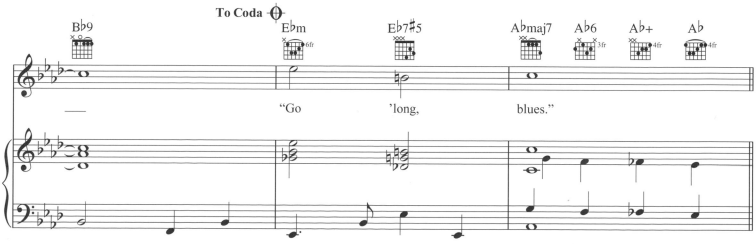

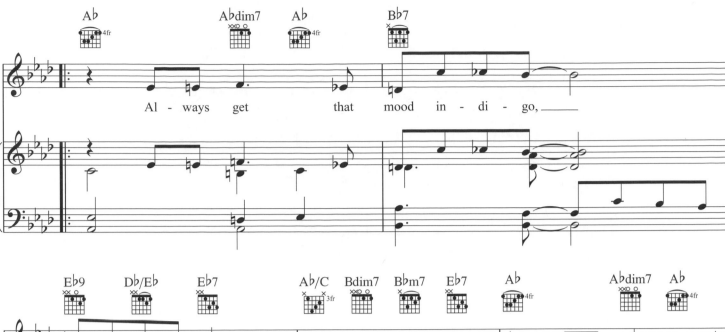

Al - ways get that mood in - di - go, ____

since my ba - by said good - bye. In the eve - nin'

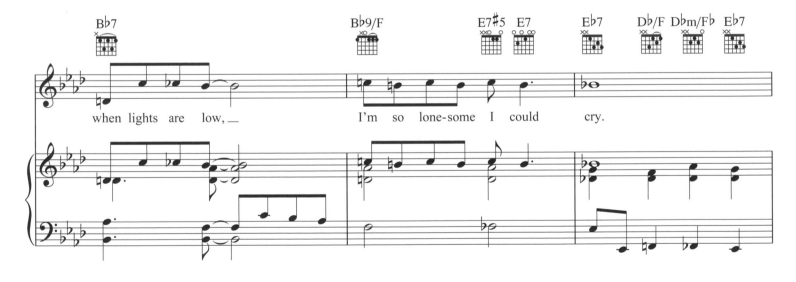

when lights are low, _ I'm so lone-some I could cry.

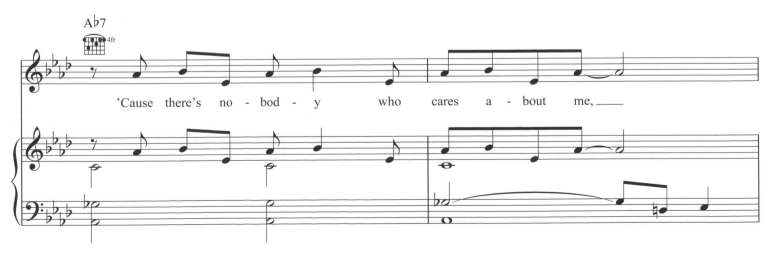

'Cause there's no - bod - y who cares a - bout me, ____

I'm just a soul who's blu-er than blue ____ can be.

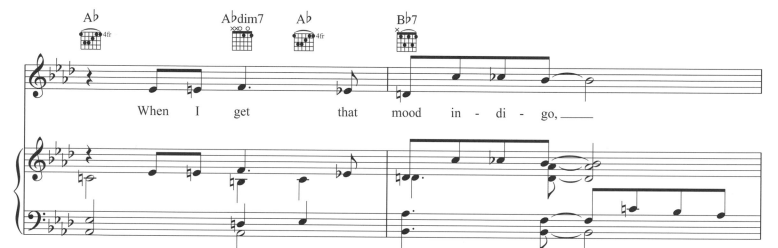

When I get that mood in-di-go, ____

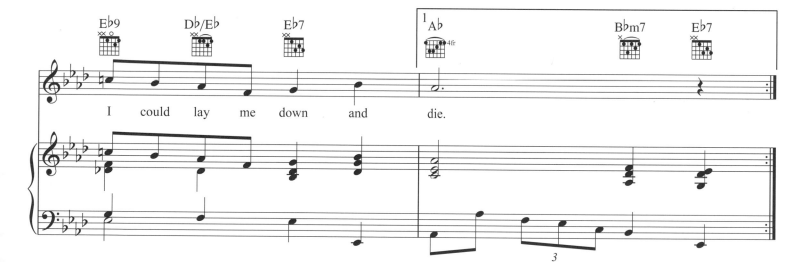

I could lay me down and die.

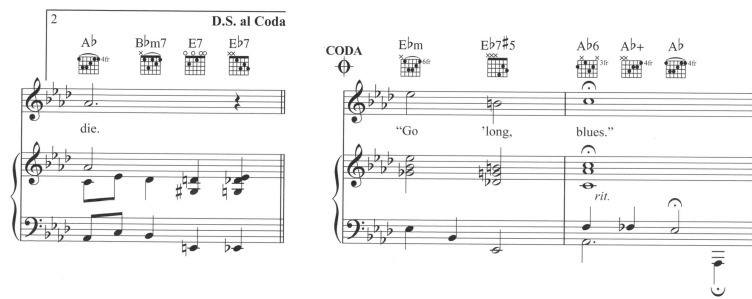

die.

"Go 'long, blues."

MOONGLOW

Words and Music by WILL HUDSON,
EDDIE DE LANGE and IRVING MILLS

It must have been Moon-glow, 'way up in the

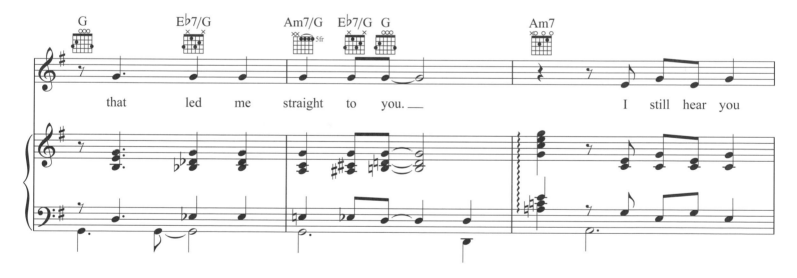

blue. It must have been Moon-glow

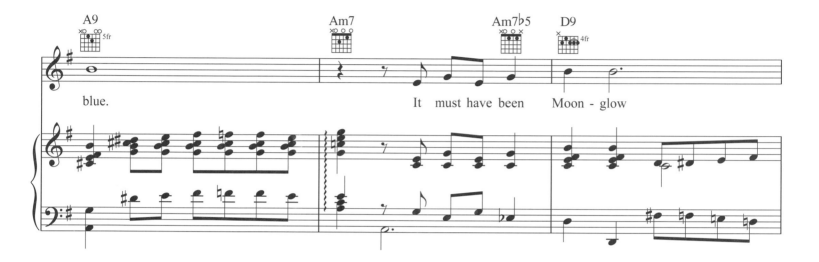

that led me straight to you. __ I still hear you

say-ing, "Dear one, hold me fast."

And I start in pray - ing, Oh Lord, please

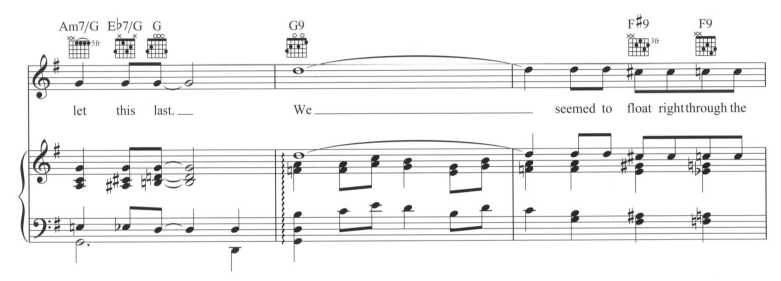

let this last. ___ We ___ seemed to float right through the

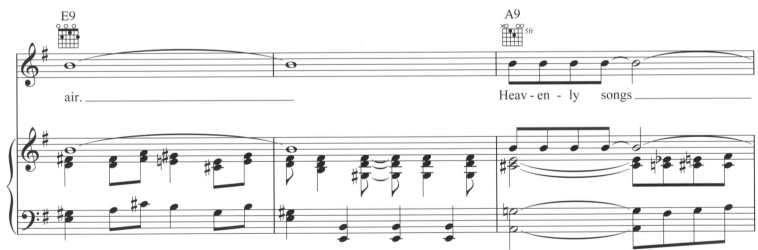

air. ___ Heav - en - ly songs ___

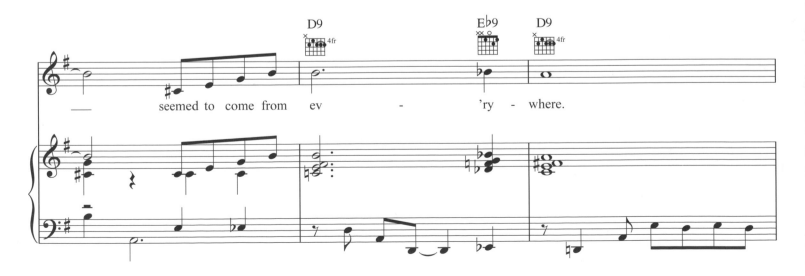

___ seemed to come from ev - 'ry - where.

MOONLIGHT SERENADE

Words by MITCHELL PARISH
Music by GLENN MILLER

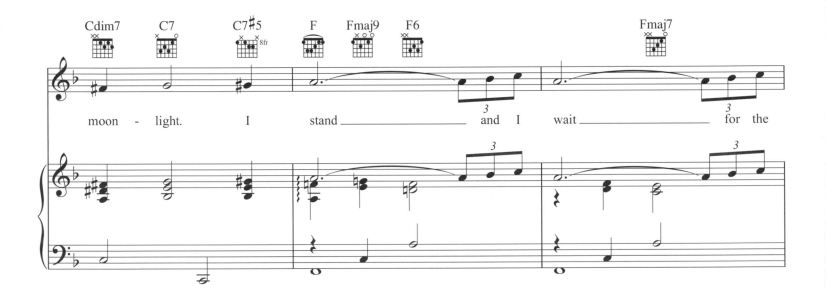

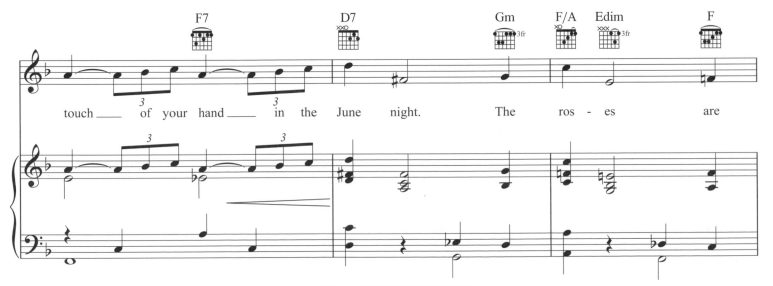

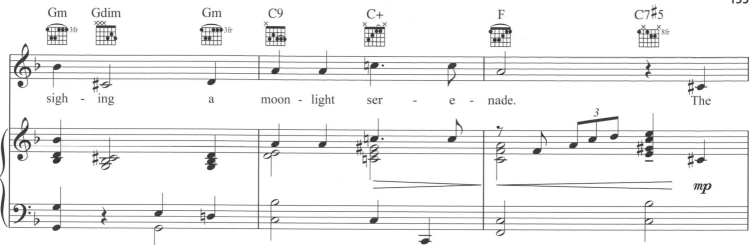

sigh-ing a moon-light ser - e - nade. The

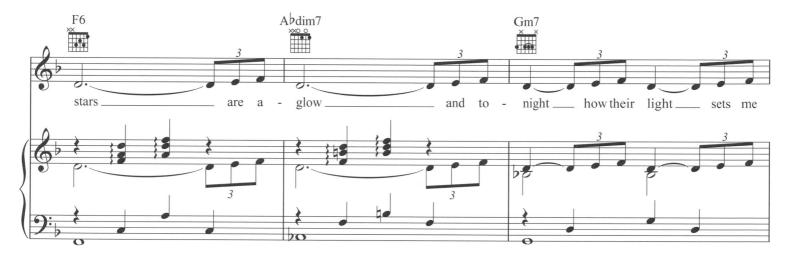

stars _____ are a - glow _____ and to - night _____ how their light _____ sets me

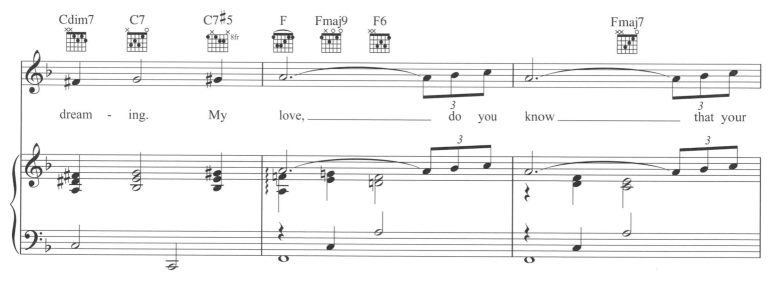

dream - ing. My love, _____ do you know _____ that your

eyes _____ are like stars _____ bright-ly beam-ing? I bring you and

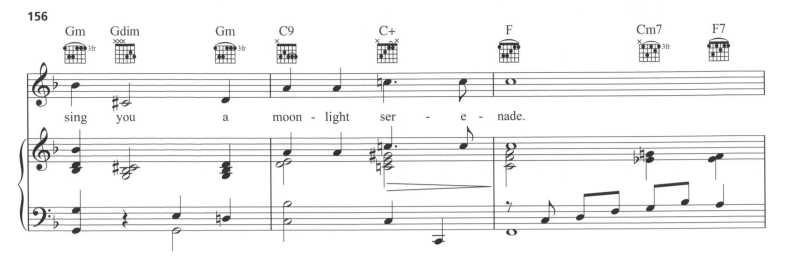

sing you a moon - light ser - e - nade.

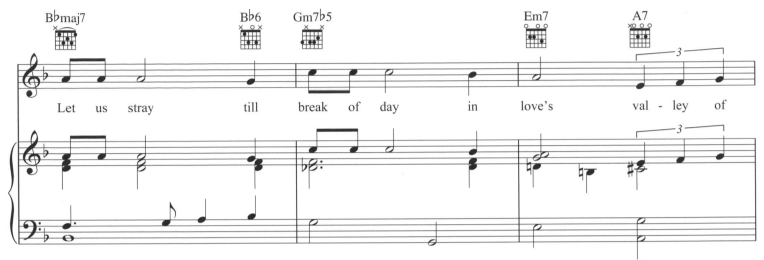

Let us stray till break of day in love's val - ley of

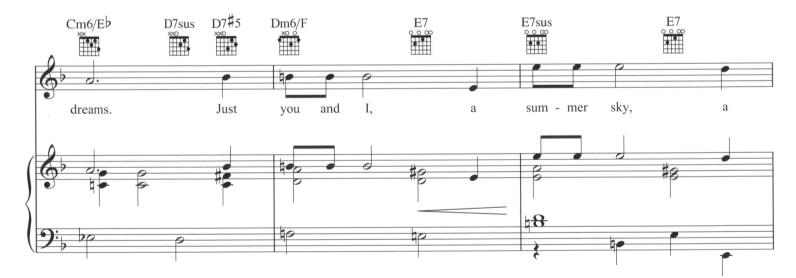

dreams. Just you and I, a sum - mer sky, a

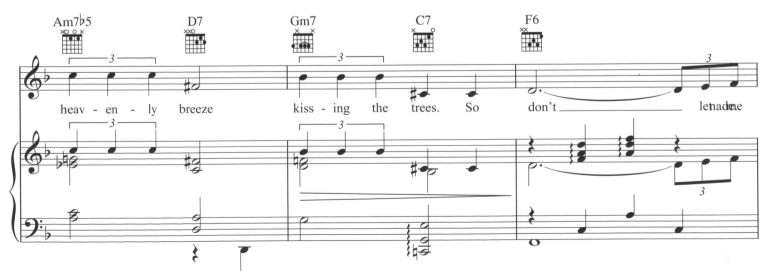

heav - en - ly breeze kiss - ing the trees. So don't _____ let me

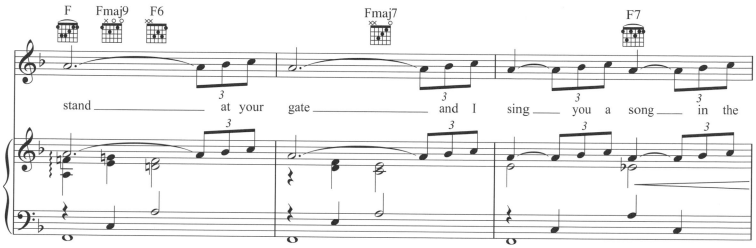

MY ROMANCE

from JUMBO

Words by LORENZ HART
Music by RICHARD RODGERS

I won't kiss your hand, Ma - dam,
cra - zy for you though I am. I'll nev - er woo you on
bend - ed knee, no, Ma - dam, not me.

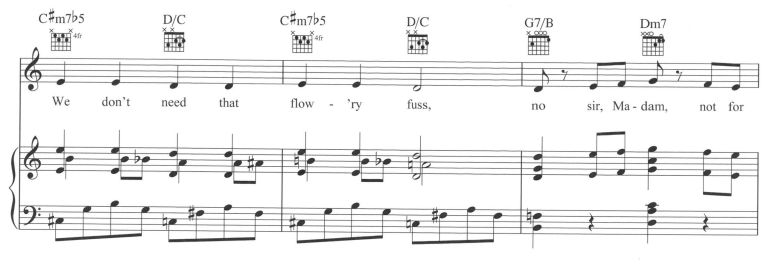

We don't need that flow - 'ry fuss, no sir, Ma - dam, not for

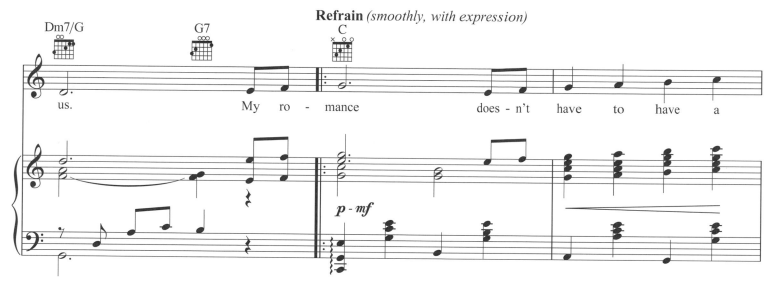

Refrain *(smoothly, with expression)*

us. My ro - mance does - n't have to have a

moon in the sky, my ro - mance does - n't

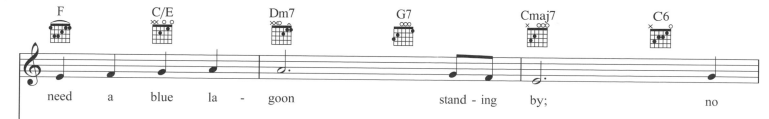

need a blue la - goon stand - ing by; no

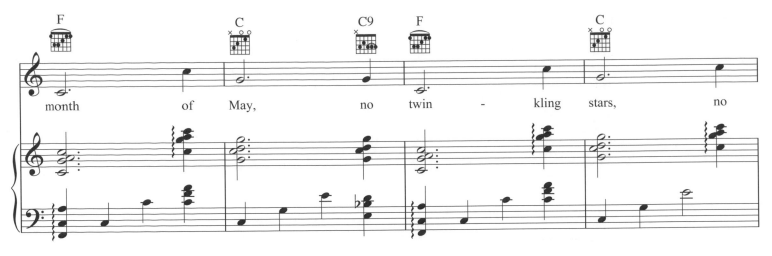

month of May, no twin - kling stars, no

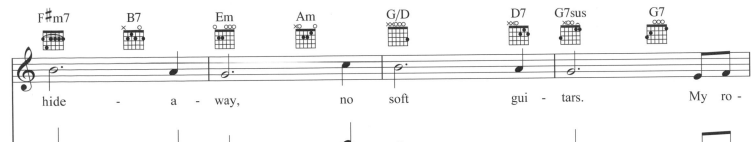

hide - a - way, no soft gui - tars. My ro -

mance does - n't need a cas - tle ris - ing in

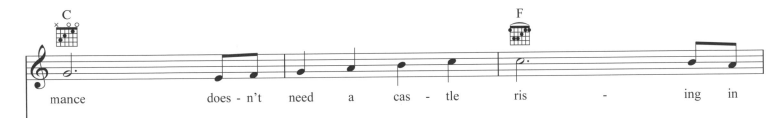

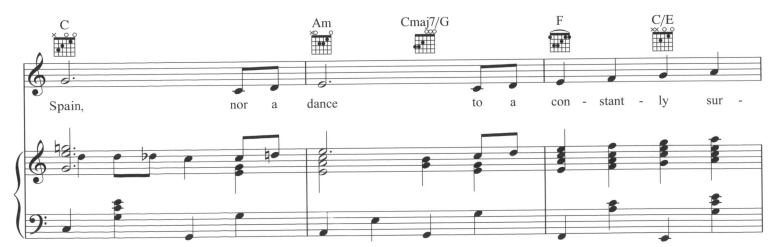

Spain, nor a dance to a con - stant - ly sur -

THE NEARNESS OF YOU

from the Paramount Picture ROMANCE IN THE DARK

Words by NED WASHINGTON
Music by HOAGY CARMICHAEL

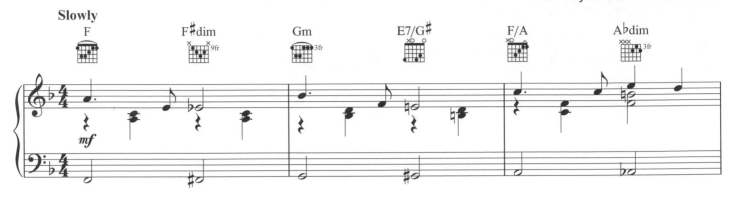

Why do I just with-er and for-get all re-sist-ance when you and your mag-ic pass

by? My heart's in a dith-er, dear, when

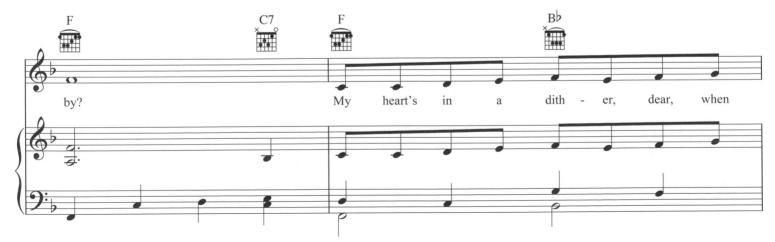

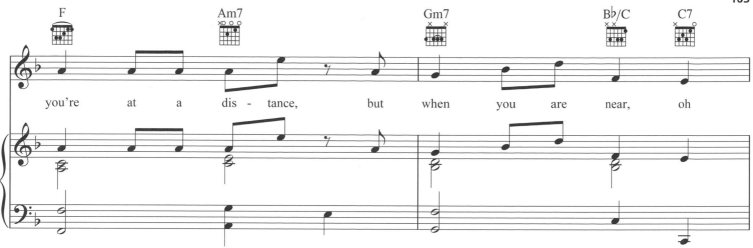

you're at a dis - tance, but when you are near, oh

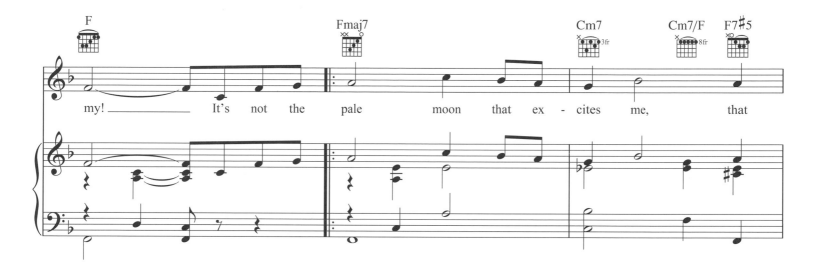

my! _____ It's not the pale moon that ex - cites me, that

thrills and de - lights me. Oh, no, _____

it's just the near - ness of you. _____

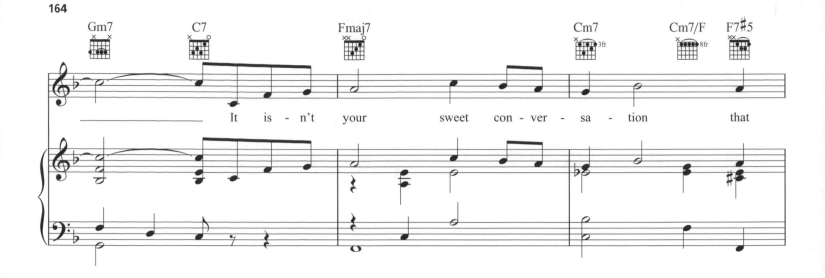

It is - n't your sweet con - ver - sa - tion that

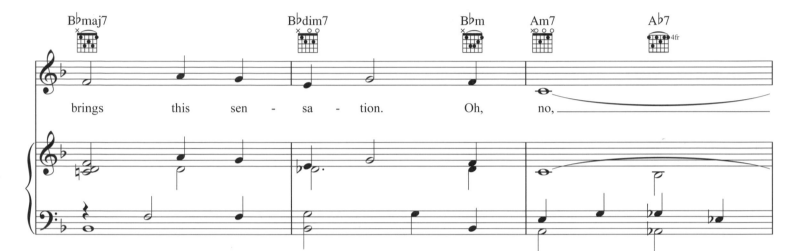

brings this sen - sa - tion. Oh, no, _____

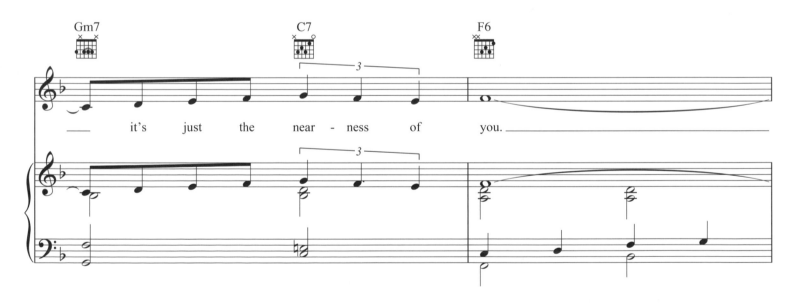

_____ it's just the near - ness of you. _____

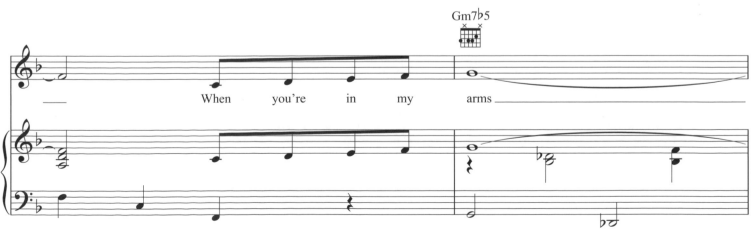

_____ When you're in my arms _____

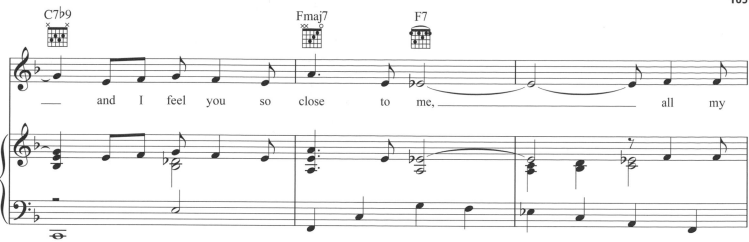

and I feel you so close to me, all my

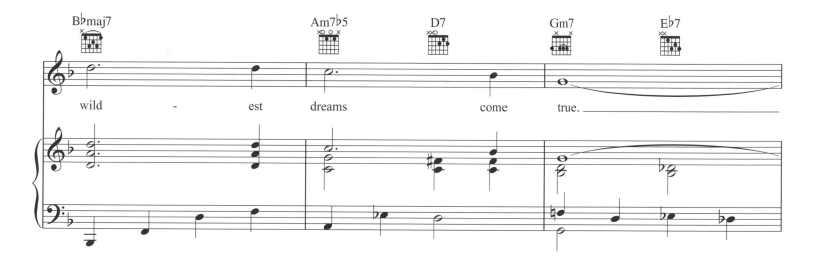

wild - est dreams come true.

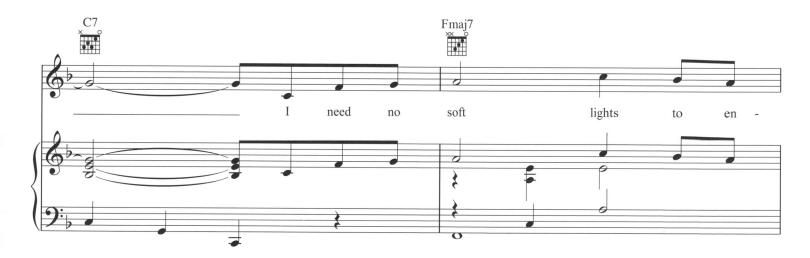

I need no soft lights to en -

chant me if you'll on - ly grant me the

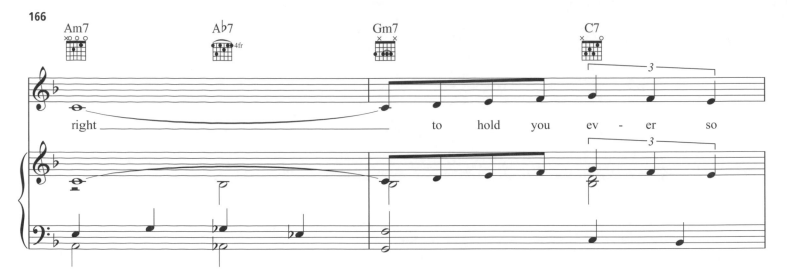

right _____ to hold you ev - er so

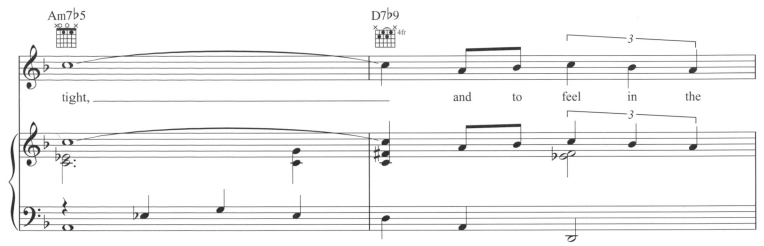

tight, _____ and to feel in the

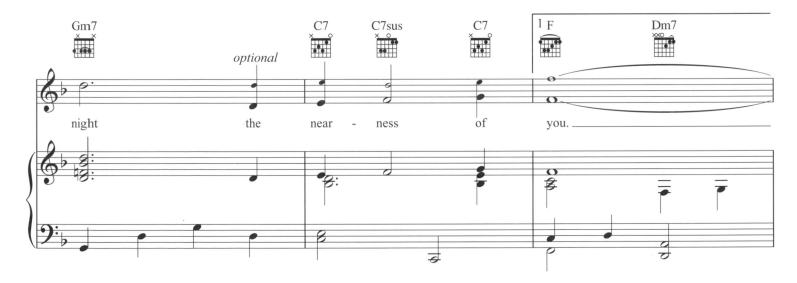

night the near - ness of you. _____

optional

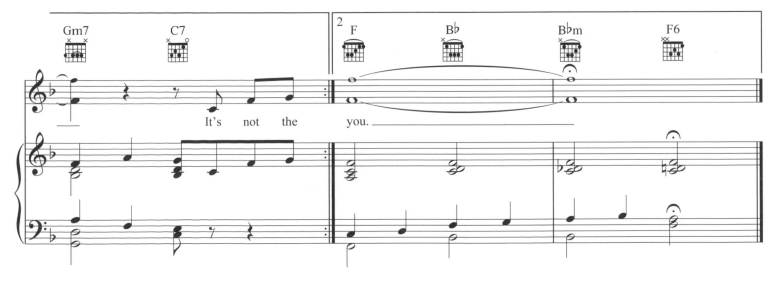

It's not the you. _____

A NIGHTINGALE SANG IN BERKELEY SQUARE

Lyric by ERIC MASCHWITZ
Music by MANNING SHERWIN

When true lov-ers meet in May-fair, so the leg-ends tell,

song - birds sing, win - ter turns to spring,

ev - 'ry wind - ing street in May - fair falls be - neath the spell. I

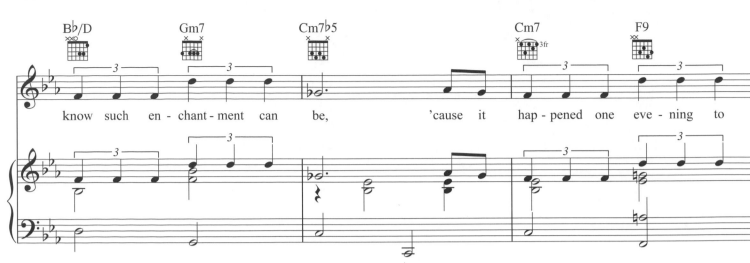

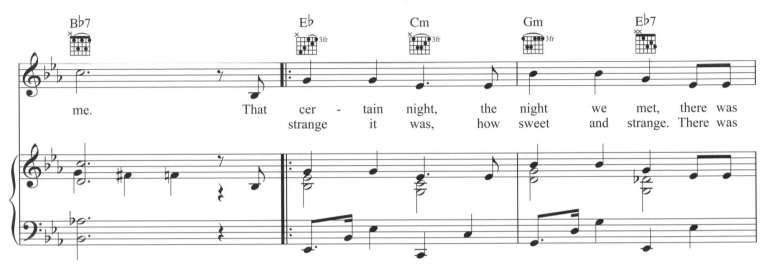

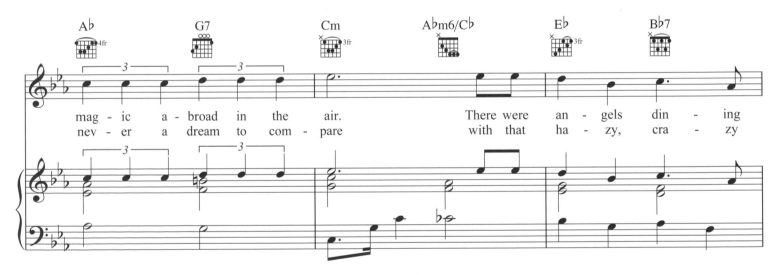

Pronounced "Bar-kley"

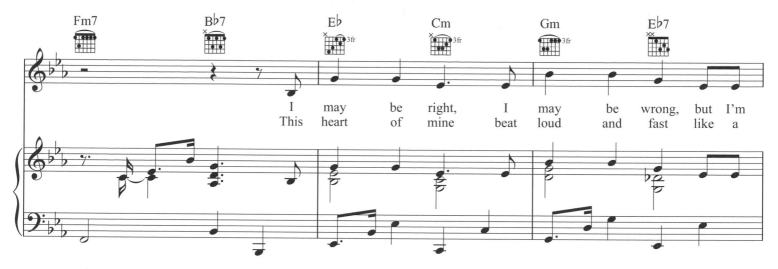

I may be right, I may be wrong, but I'm
This heart of mine beat loud and fast like a

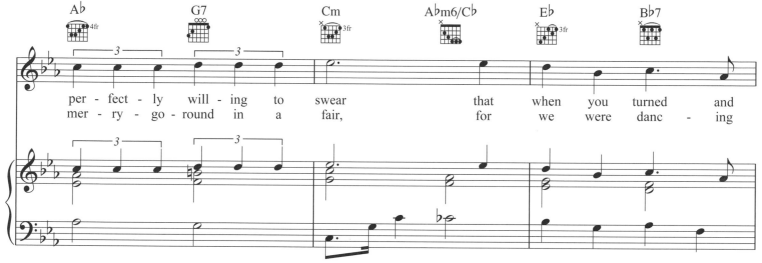

per - fect - ly will - ing to swear that when you turned and
mer - ry - go - round in a fair, for we were danc - ing

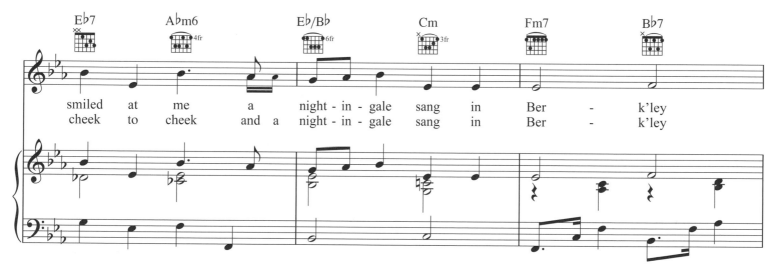

smiled at me a night - in - gale sang in Ber - k'ley
cheek to cheek and a night - in - gale sang in Ber - k'ley

Square. The moon that lin - gered o - ver
Square. When dawn came steal - ing up all

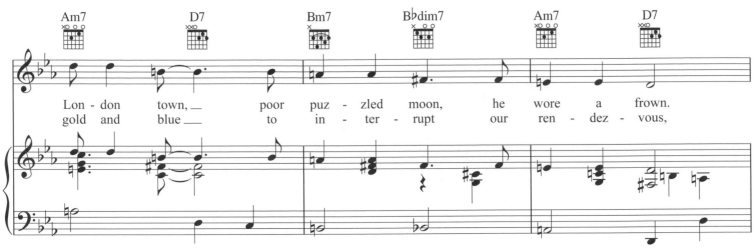

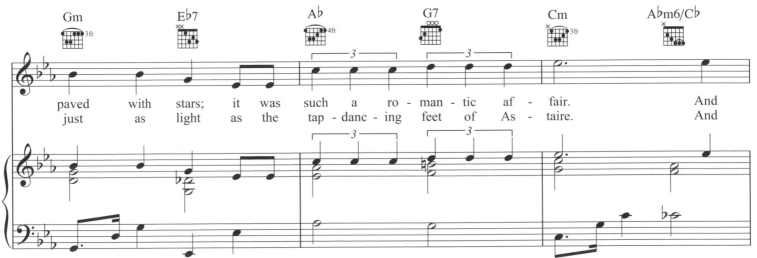

as we kissed and said "good-night," a night-in-gale sang in
like an ech-o far a-way, a night-in-gale sang in

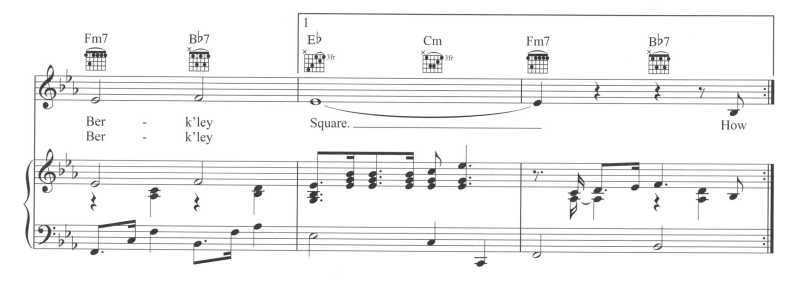

Ber - k'ley Square.____ How
Ber - k'ley

Square.

I know 'cause I was there

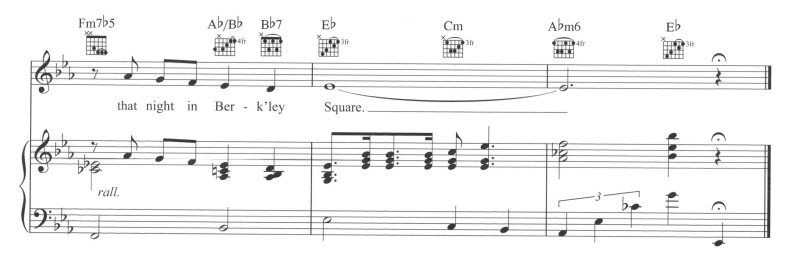

that night in Ber - k'ley Square.____

ON THE SUNNY SIDE OF THE STREET

Lyric by DOROTHY FIELDS
Music by JIMMY McHUGH

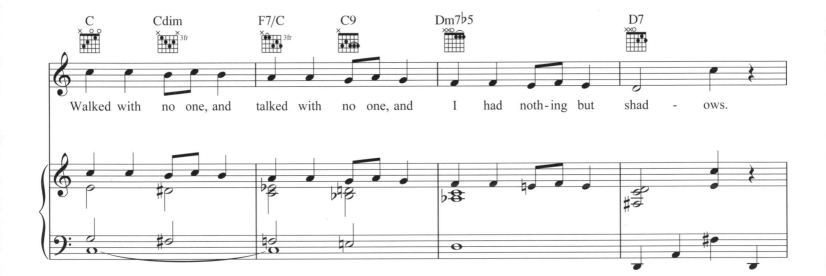

Walked with no one, and talked with no one, and I had noth-ing but shad - ows.

Then one morn-ing you passed, and I bright-ened at last.

Now I greet the day and com-plete the day with the sun in my

heart. All my wor-ry blew a-way

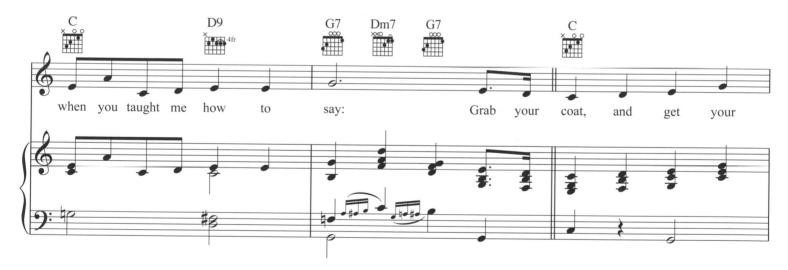

when you taught me how to say: Grab your coat, and get your

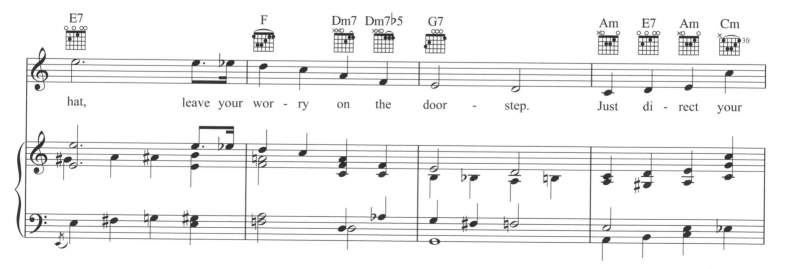

hat, leave your wor-ry on the door-step. Just di-rect your

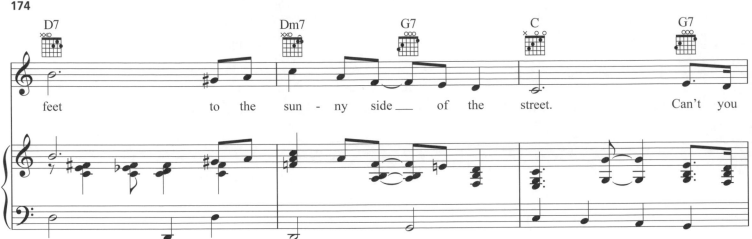

feet to the sun - ny side ___ of the street. Can't you

hear a pit - ter - pat? And that hap - py tune is

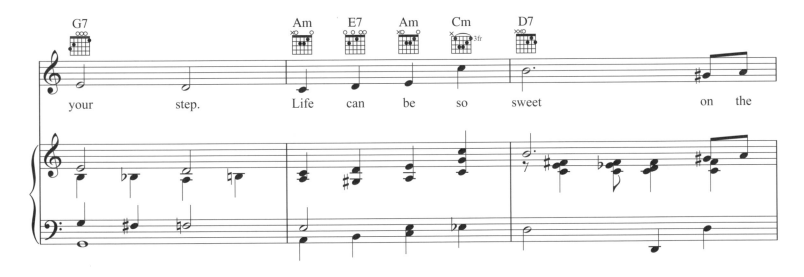

your step. Life can be so sweet on the

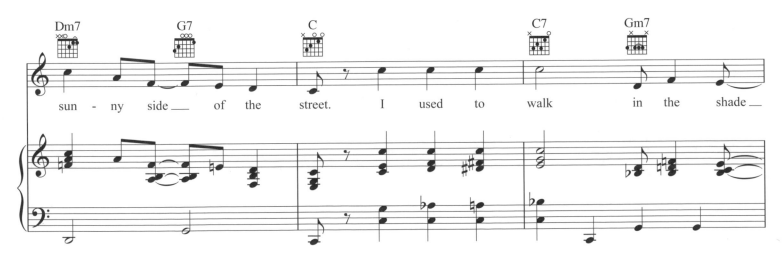

sun - ny side ___ of the street. I used to walk in the shade ___

with those blues on pa - rade, ___ but I'm not a - fraid, ___

___ this Ro - ver crossed o - ver. If I nev - er have a

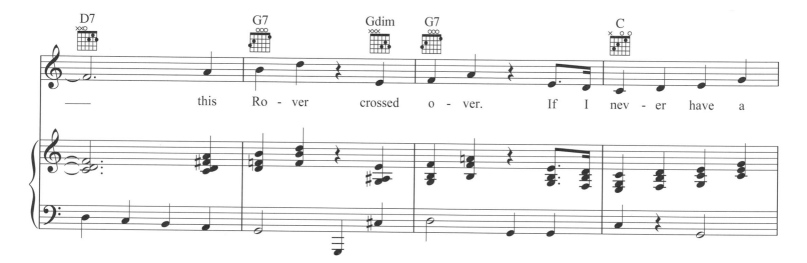

cent, I'll be rich as Rock - e - fel - ler. Gold dust at my

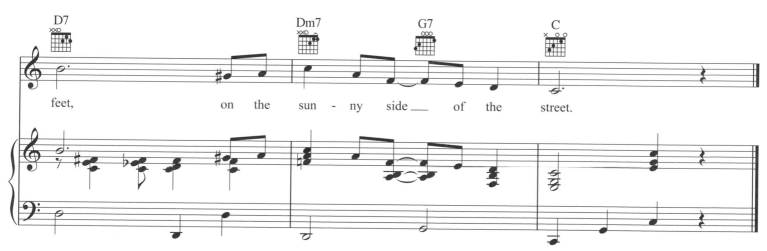

feet, on the sun - ny side ___ of the street.

ONE O'CLOCK JUMP

By COUNT BASIE

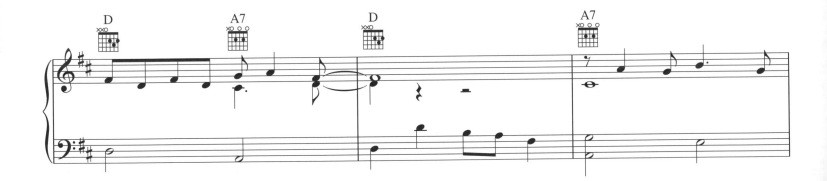

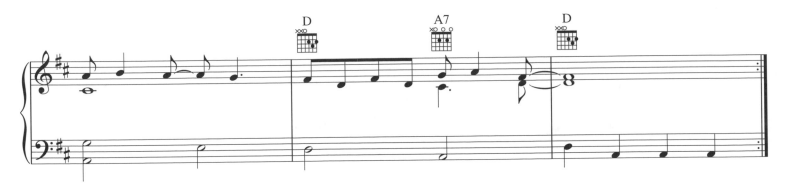

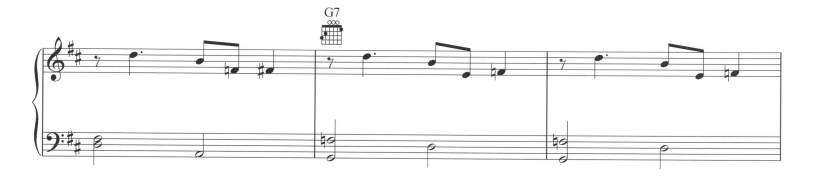

OPUS ONE

Words and Music by
SY OLIVER

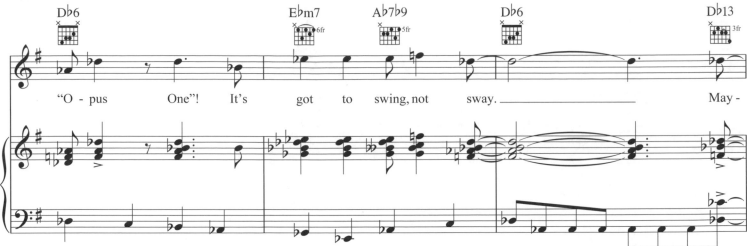

"O - pus One"! It's got to swing, not sway. _____ May-

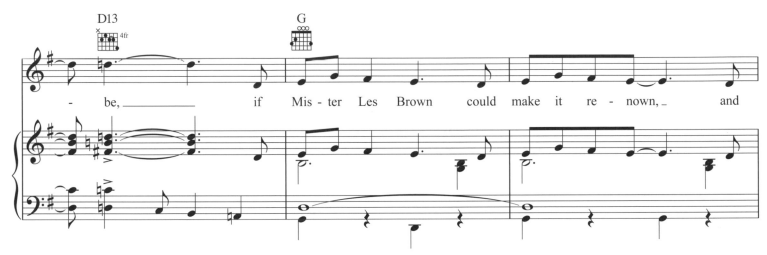

- be, _____ if Mis - ter Les Brown could make it re - nown, ___ and

Ray An - tho - ny could swing it for me, __ there's nev - er a doubt you'll knock your-self out ___ when-

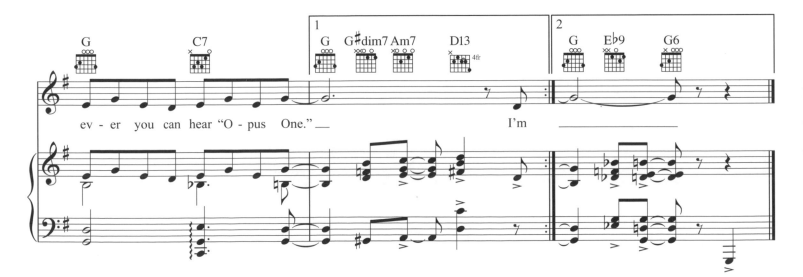

ev - er you can hear "O - pus One." ___ I'm

SATIN DOLL

Words by JOHNNY MERCER,
BILLY STRAYHORN and DUKE ELLINGTON
Music by DUKE ELLINGTON

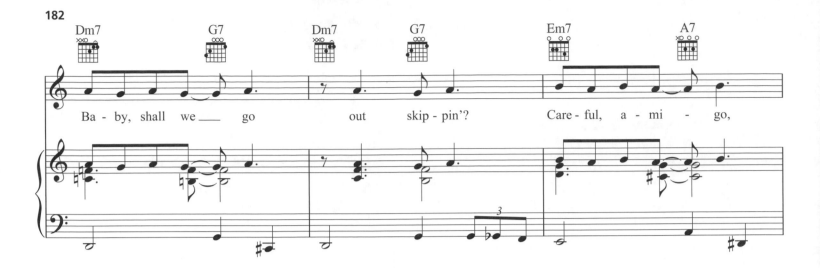

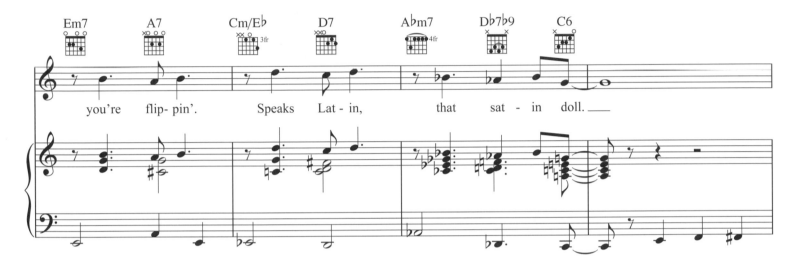

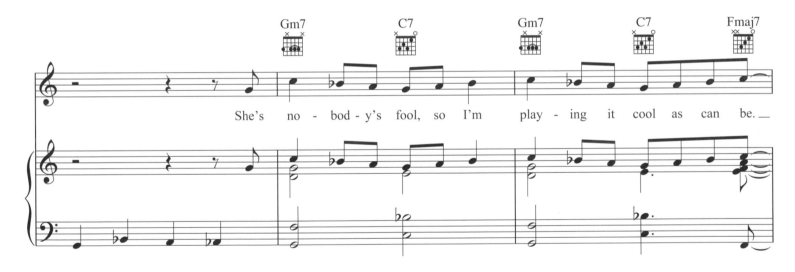

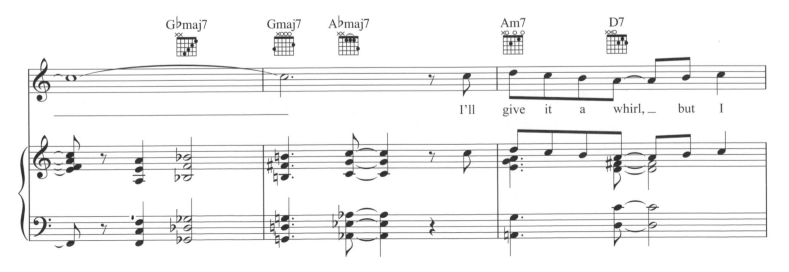

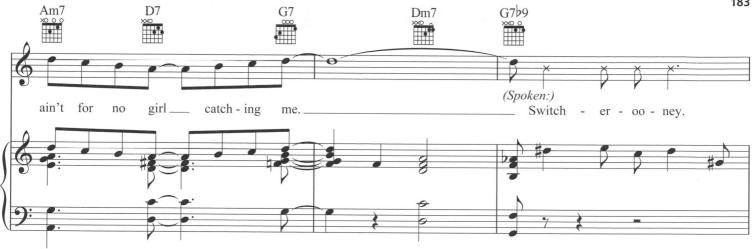

ain't for no girl ___ catch - ing me. ___ *(Spoken:)* Switch - er - oo - ney.

Tel - e - phone num - bers well you know, do - ing my rhum - bas

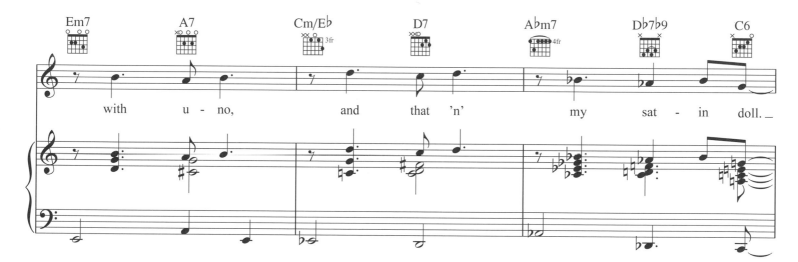

with u - no, and that 'n' my sat - in doll. ___

PENNSYLVANIA 6-5000

Words by CARL SIGMAN
Music by JERRY GRAY

Moderately, with a swing

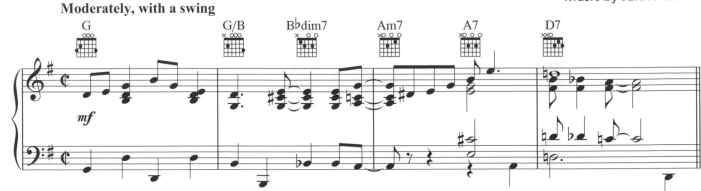

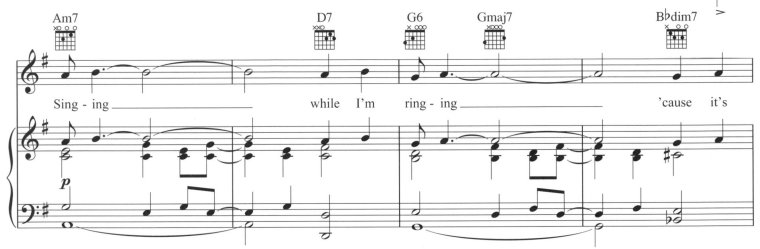

Sing-ing _____ while I'm ring-ing _____ 'cause it's

bring-ing _____ such de - light. _____

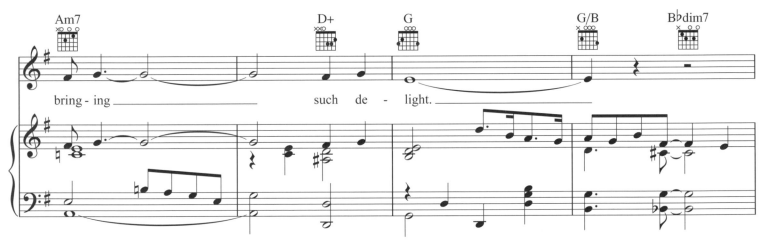

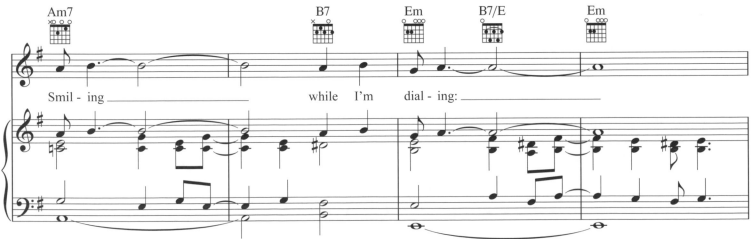

Smil-ing _____ while I'm dial-ing: _____

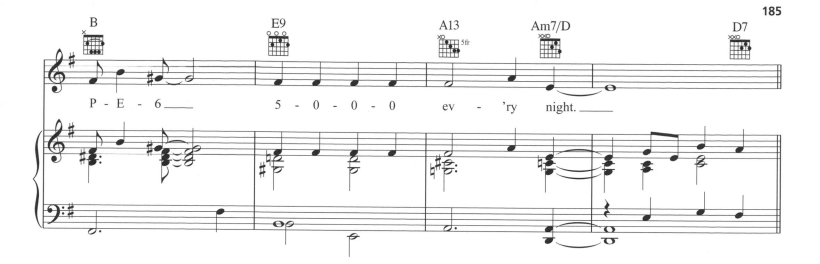

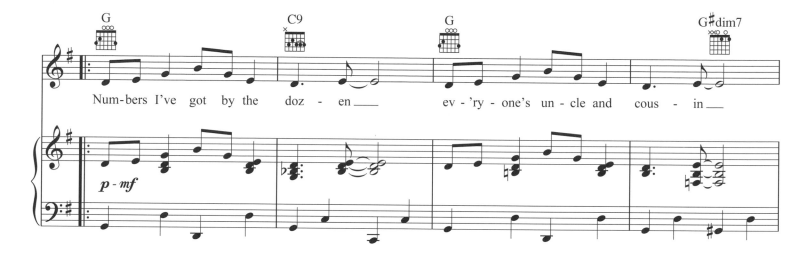

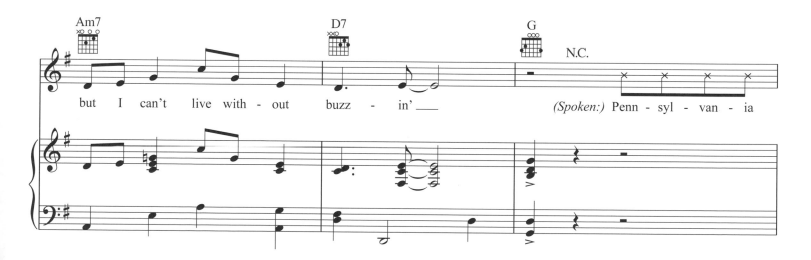

some-one who sets me a-glow there ___ gives me the sweet-est "hel-

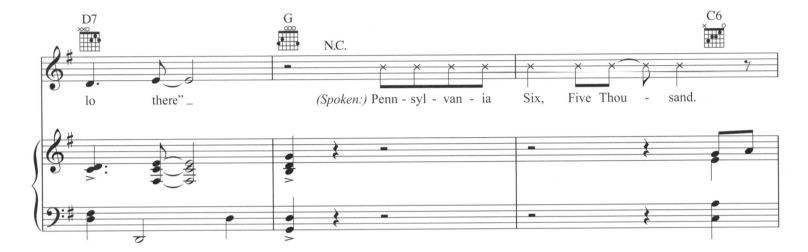

lo there" ___ *(Spoken:)* Penn-syl-van-ia Six, Five Thou-sand.

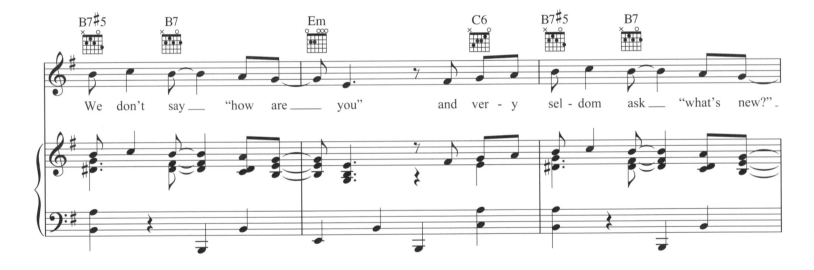

We don't say ___ "how are ___ you" and ver-y sel-dom ask ___ "what's new?" ___

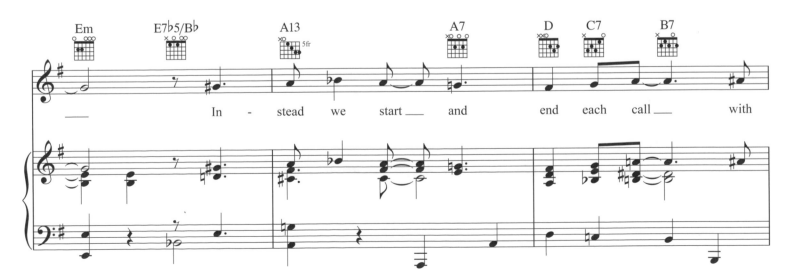

___ In-stead we start ___ and end each call ___ with

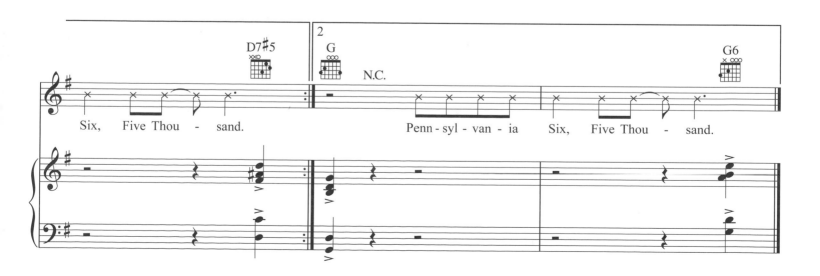

SENTIMENTAL JOURNEY

Words and Music by BUD GREEN,
LES BROWN and BEN HOMER

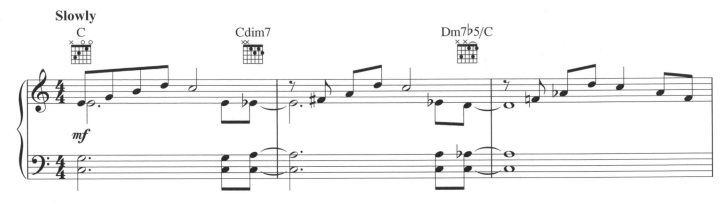

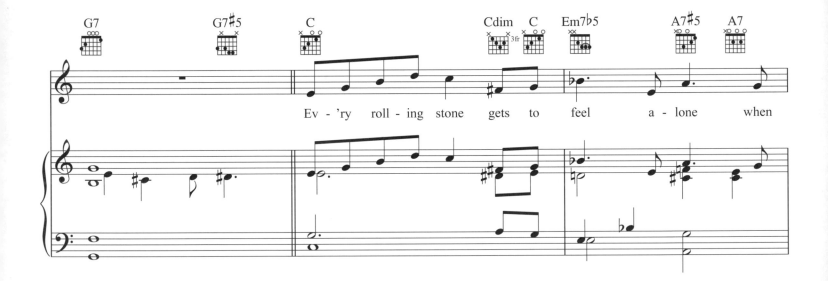

Ev - 'ry roll - ing stone gets to feel a - lone when

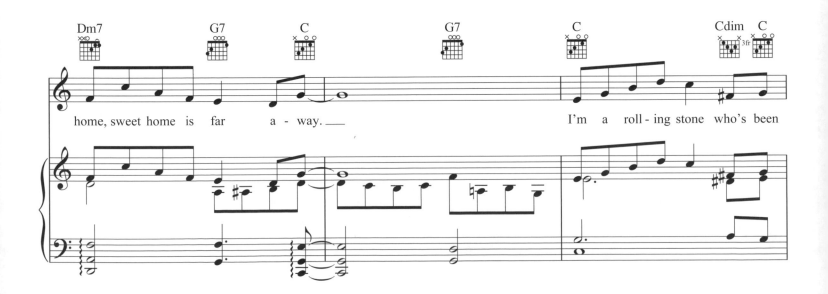

home, sweet home is far a - way. ___ I'm a roll - ing stone who's been

so a - lone un - til to - day.

Gon - na take a sen - ti - men - tal jour - ney, gon - na set my

heart at ease. ___ Gon - na make a sen - ti - men - tal jour - ney

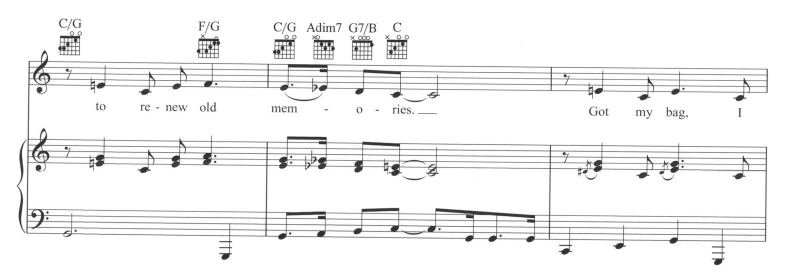

to re - new old mem - o - ries. ___ Got my bag, I

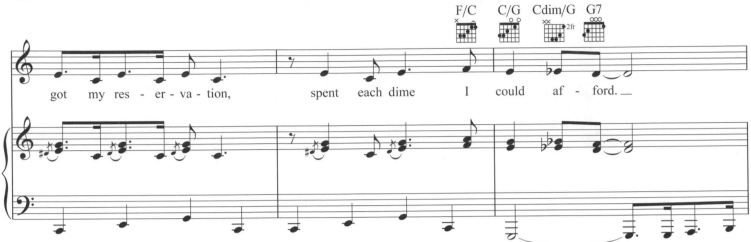

got my res - er - va - tion, spent each dime I could af - ford.

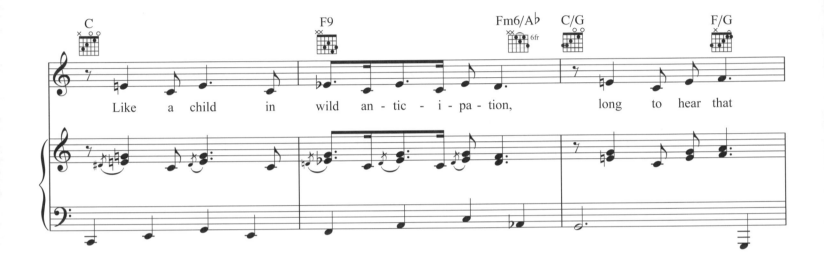

Like a child in wild an - tic - i - pa - tion, long to hear that

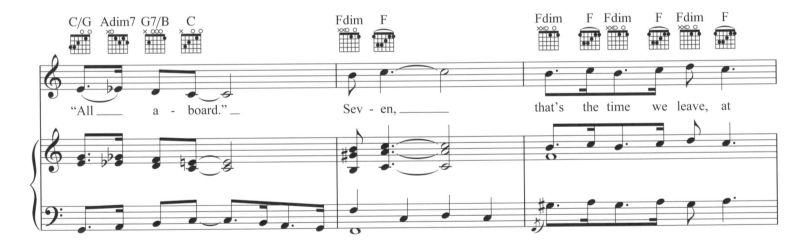

"All ___ a - board." ___ Sev - en, ___ that's the time we leave, at

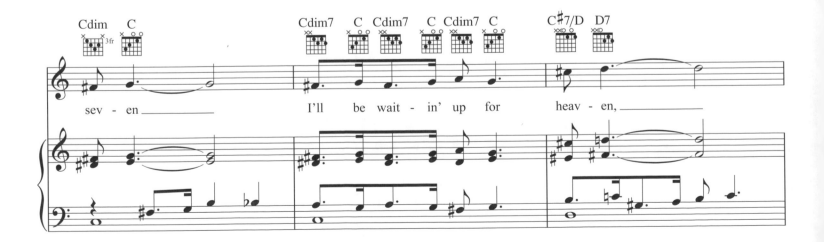

sev - en ___ I'll be wait - in' up for heav - en, ___

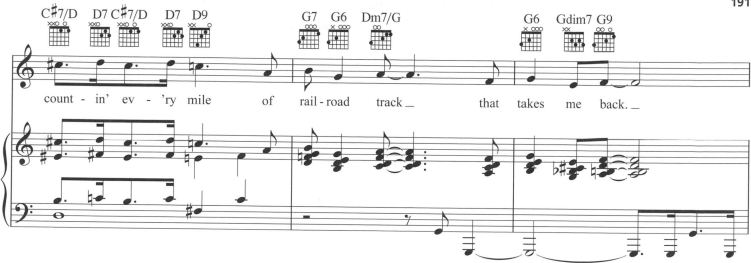

count - in' ev - 'ry mile of rail - road track __ that takes me back. __

Nev - er thought my heart could be so "yearn - y." Why did I de -

cide to roam? __ Got - ta take a sen - ti - men - tal jour - ney,

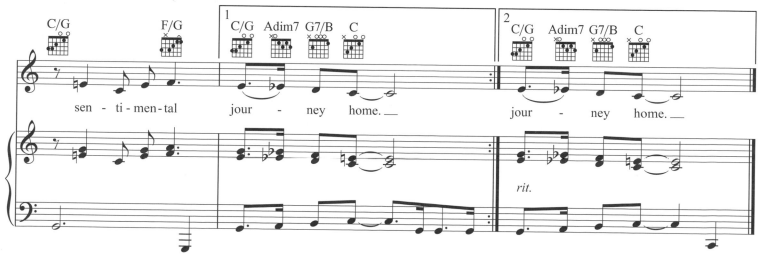

sen - ti - men - tal jour - ney home. __ jour - ney home. __

SHINY STOCKINGS

Words by ELLA FITZGERALD
Music by FRANK FOSTER

SING, SING, SING

Words and Music by
LOUIS PRIMA

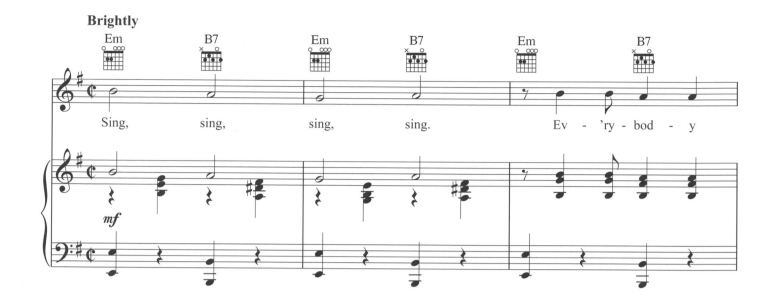

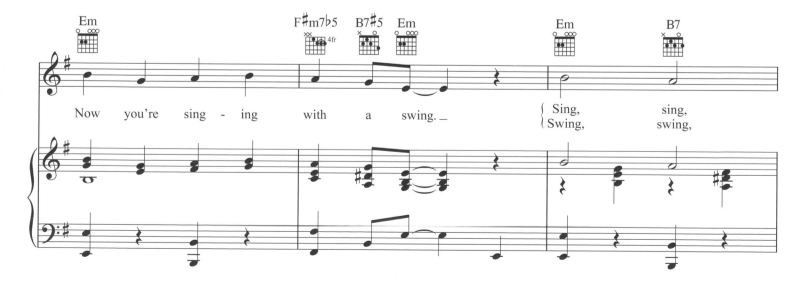

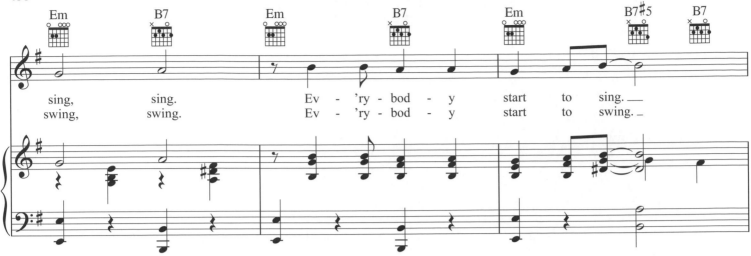

sing,   sing.   Ev – 'ry-bod – y start to sing. __

swing,   swing.   Ev – 'ry-bod – y start to swing. __

La – dle – la,   whoa – ho – ho.   Now you're sing – ing

La – dle – la,   whoa – ho – ho.   Now you're swing – in'

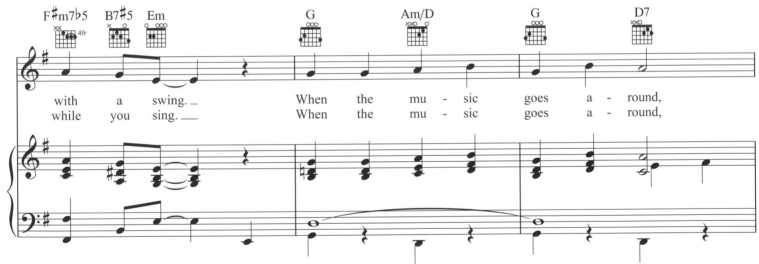

with a swing. __   When the mu – sic goes a – round,

while you sing. __   When the mu – sic goes a – round,

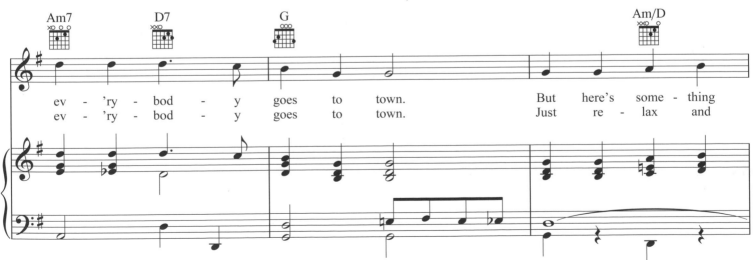

ev – 'ry-bod – y goes to town.   But here's some – thing

ev – 'ry-bod – y goes to town.   Just re – lax and

you should know. Ho - ho, ba - by, ho - ho - ho.
take it slow. Ho - ho, ba - by, ho - ho - ho. }

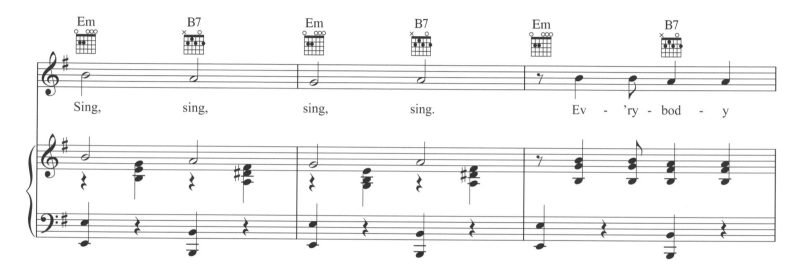

Sing, sing, sing, sing. Ev - 'ry - bod - y

start to sing. La - dle - la, whoa - ho - ho.

Now you're sing - ing with a swing. with a swing.

SKYLINER

Words and Music by
CHARLIE BARNET

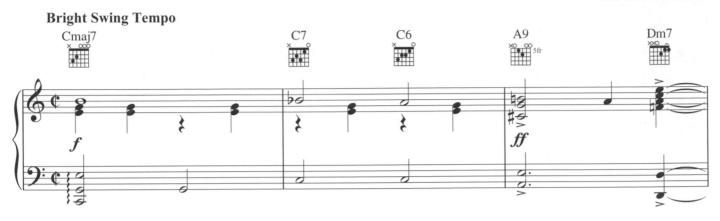

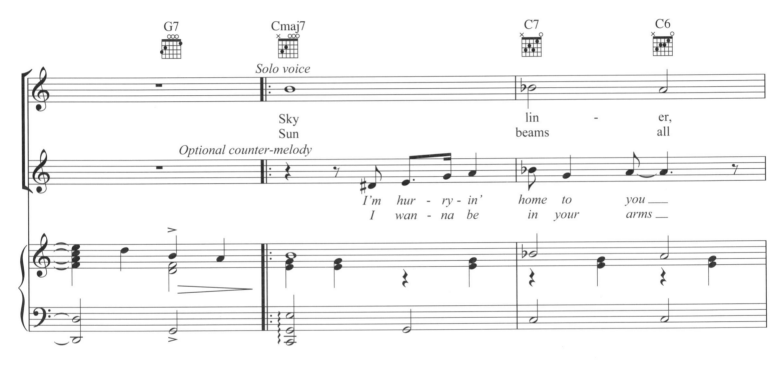

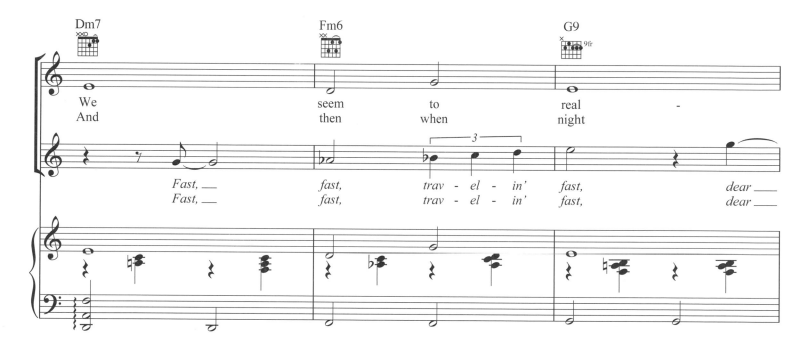

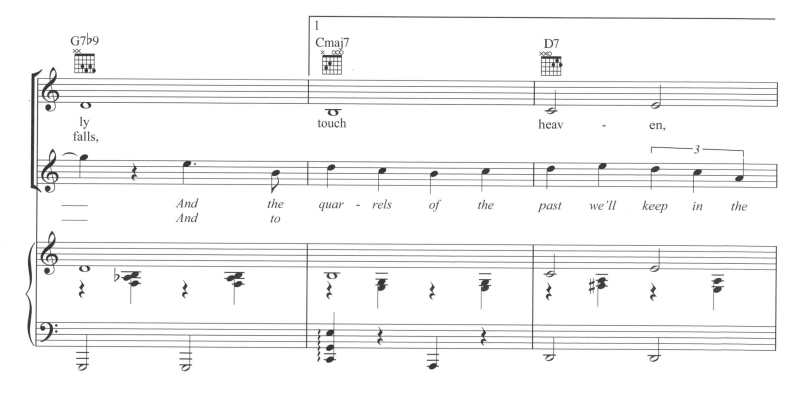

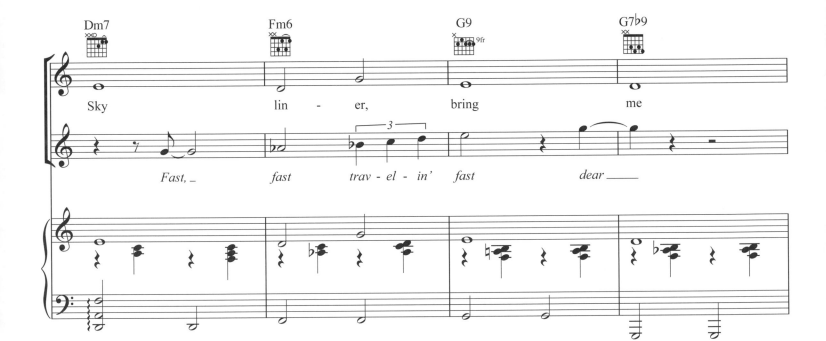

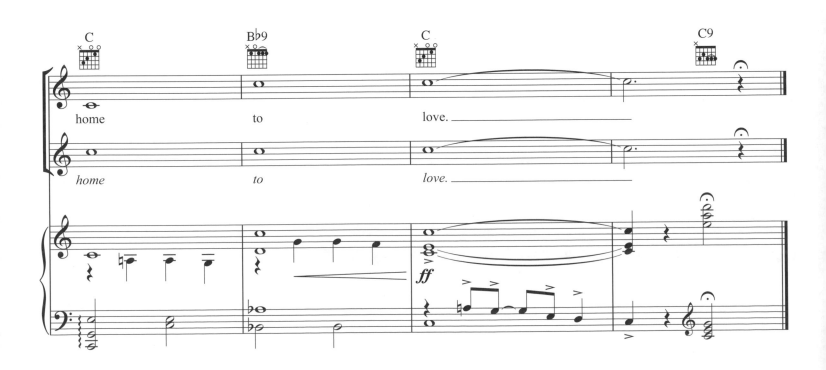

STARDUST

Words by MITCHELL PARISH
Music by HOAGY CARMICHAEL

But that was long a-go: now my con-so-la-tion is

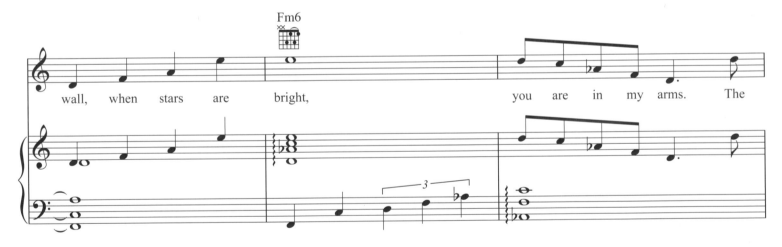

in the star-dust of a song. Be-side a gar-den

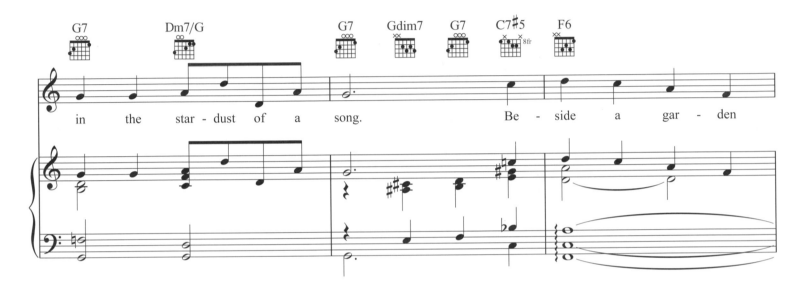

wall, when stars are bright, you are in my arms. The

night-in-gale tells his fair-y tale of par-a-dise, where ros-es

SOMEBODY LOVES YOU

Words by CHARLIE TOBIAS
Music by PETER DE ROSE

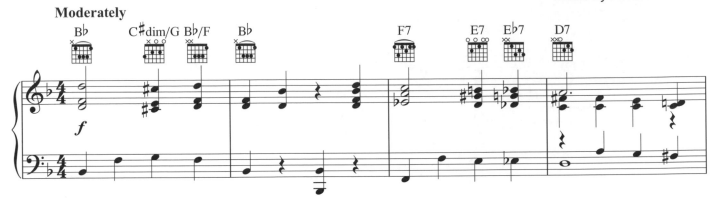

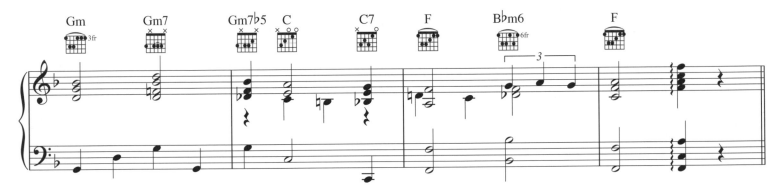

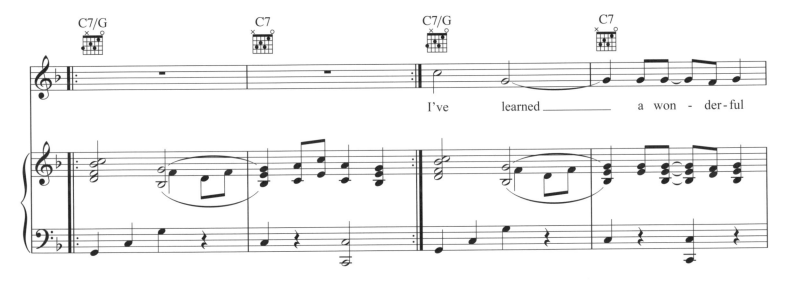

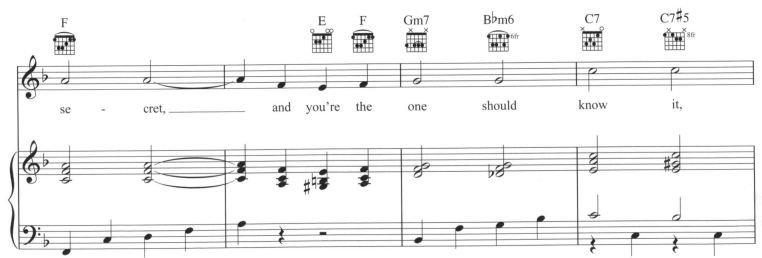

I've learned _____ a won - der - ful se - cret, _____ and you're the one should know it,

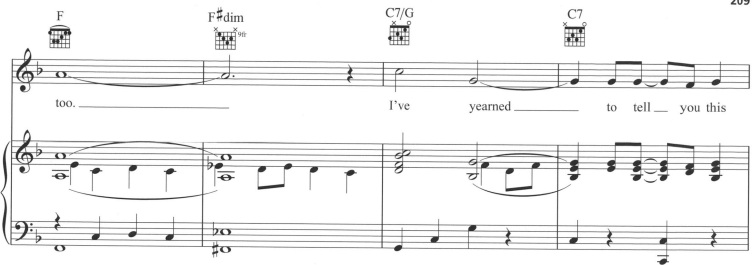

too. _____ I've yearned _____ to tell __ you this

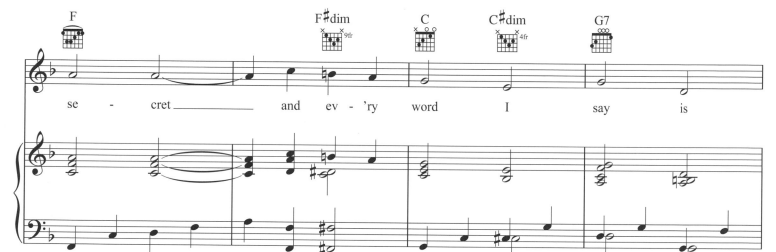

se - cret _____ and ev - 'ry word I say is

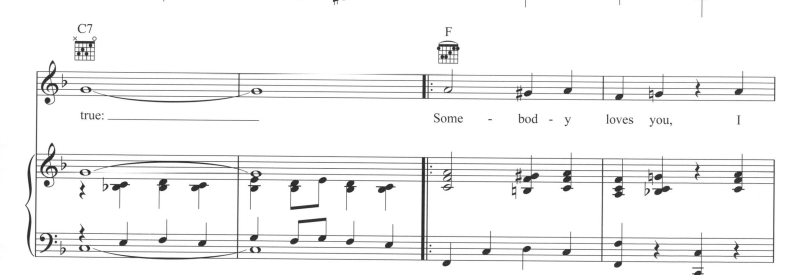

true: _____ Some - bod - y loves you, I

want you to know. Longs to be near you wher -

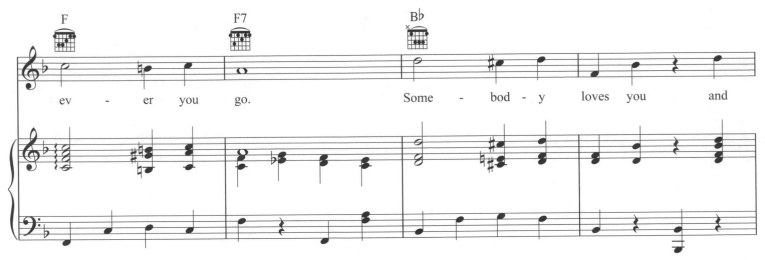

ev - er you go. Some - bod - y loves you and

right from the start, hap - pi - ness flew in - to

some - one's heart; _____ Some - bod - y

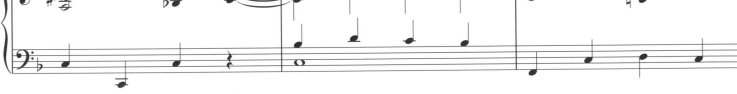

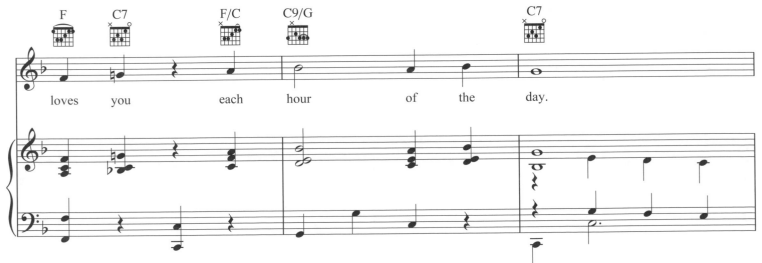

loves you each hour of the day.

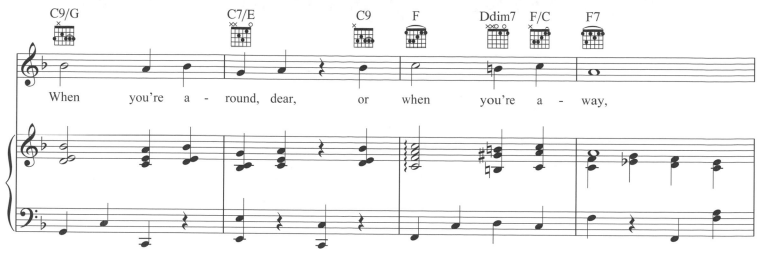

When you're a - round, dear, or when you're a - way,

some - bod - y loves you, sweet - heart, can't you

see? And that some - bod - y is

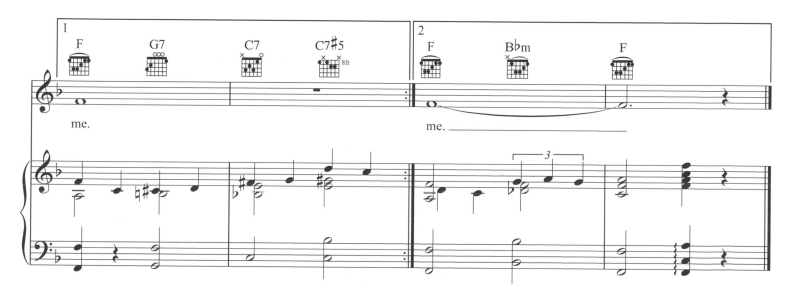

1. me.

2. me. _____

STRAIGHTEN UP AND FLY RIGHT

Words and Music by NAT KING COLE
and IRVING MILLS

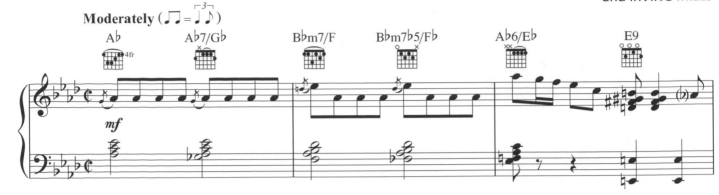

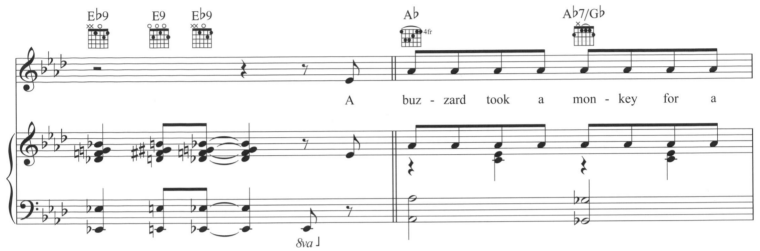

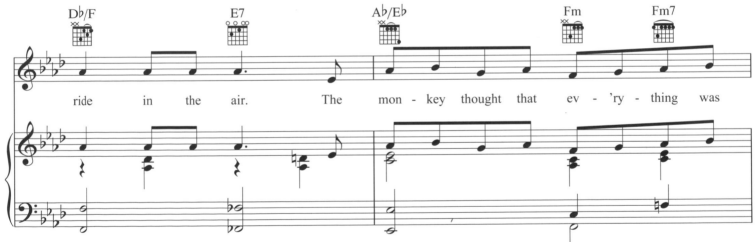

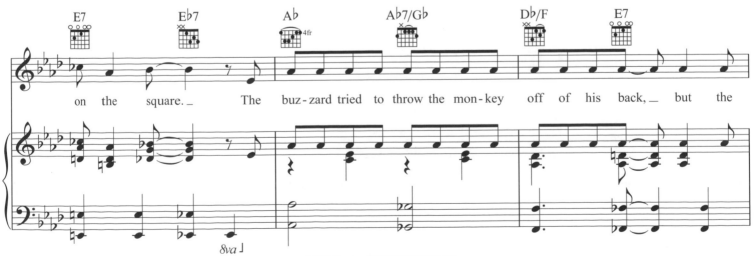

mon - key grabbed his neck and said, "Now lis - ten, Jack!" —

Straight - en up and fly ___ right! ___ Straight - en up and fly ___

___ right! ___ Straight - en up and fly ___ right! ___ Cool ___

___ down, Pa - pa, don't you blow your top. ___ Ain't no use in div -

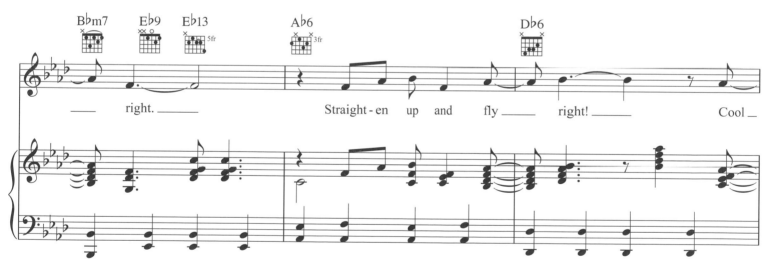

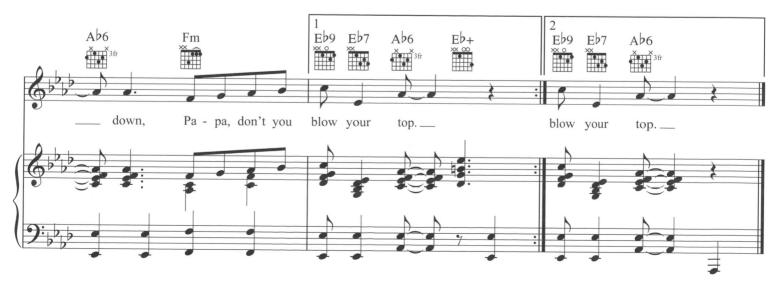

A STRING OF PEARLS
from THE GLENN MILLER STORY

Words by EDDIE DE LANGE
Music by JERRY GRAY

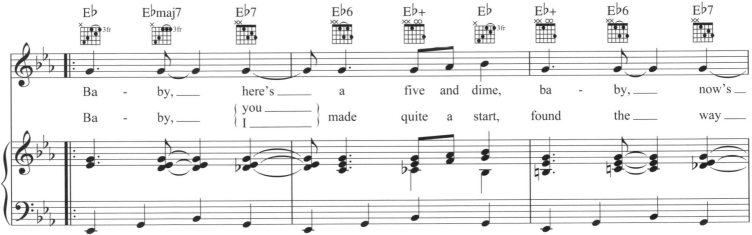

Ba - by, ___ here's ___ a five and dime, ba - by, ___ now's ___
Ba - by, ___ { you ___ / I ___ } made quite a start, found the ___ way ___

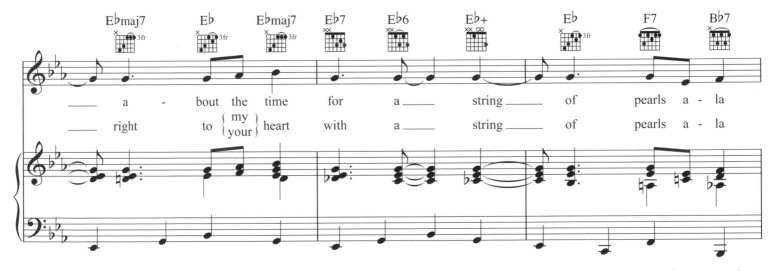

___ a - bout the time for a ___ string ___ of pearls a - la
___ right to { my / your } heart with a ___ string ___ of pearls a - la

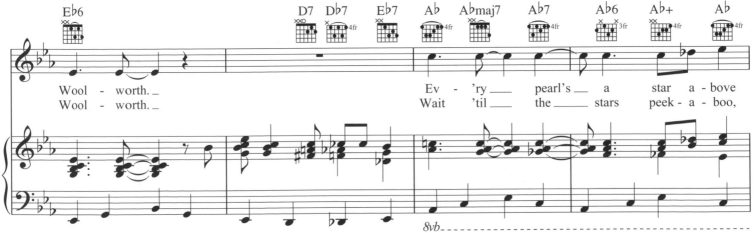

Wool - worth. ___ Ev - 'ry ___ pearl's ___ a star a - bove
Wool - worth. ___ Wait 'til ___ the ___ stars peek - a - boo,

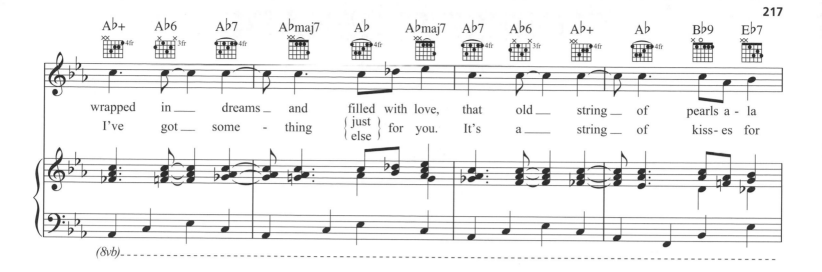

wrapped in ___ dreams ___ and filled with love, that old ___ string ___ of pearls a - la
I've got ___ some - thing { just / else } for you. It's a ___ string ___ of kiss - es for

Wool - worth. ___
ba - by. ___

'Til that ___ hap - py day in Spring
I found a ___ love so sub - lime,

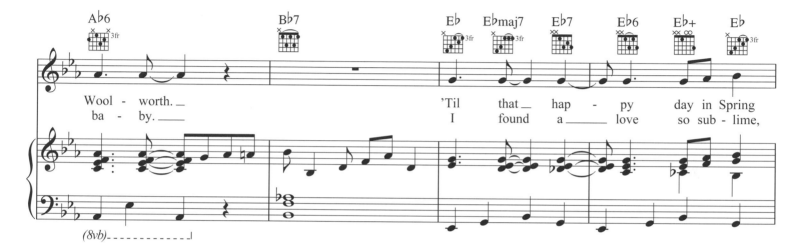

when { you ___ / I ___ } buy ___ the wed - ding ring, please, a ___ string ___ of pearls a - la
right in ___ that ___ old five and dime, with a ___ string ___ of pearls a - la

Wool - worth. ___
Wool - worth. ___

SUNRISE SERENADE

Lyric by JACK LAWRENCE
Music by FRANKIE CARLE

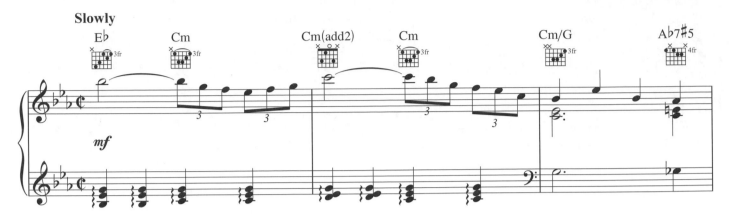

Good morn-in', good morn-in', you sleep-y-head. __ It's

dawn-in', stop yawn-in', get out of that bed. __ Say the air is soft as silk, __ it's time to

get the morn-in' milk. Come on! ___ Wake up! ___ Get up! ___ Look at the grass, ___

___ sil - ver in the sun, ___ heav - y with the dew. _____ Look at the buds, ___

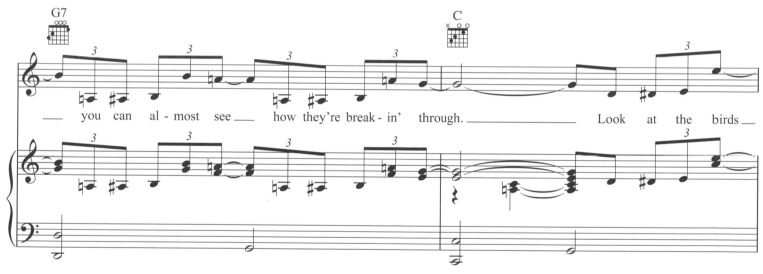

___ you can al - most see ___ how they're break - in' through. _____ Look at the birds ___

___ feed-in' all their young ___ in the syc - a - mores. _____ But you bet - ter get on with your morn - in'

chores. _____ Just take a breath ___ of that new-mown hay ___ and the sug - ar cane. ___

_____ Looks like to - night ___ there should be a moon ___ down in Lov - er's Lane. ___

_____ There you go day - dream - ing when it's time that you o - beyed that sun -

- rise ser - e - nade. _____ Good ___

TAKE THE "A" TRAIN

Words and Music by
BILLY STRAYHORN

Moderately fast Swing

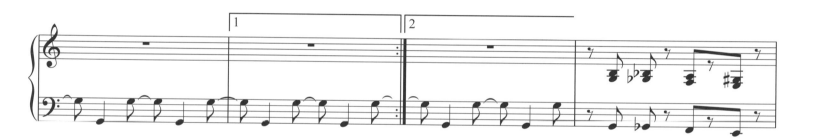

Fine

You   must   take   the   "A" _____   train _____

to go to Sug - ar Hill way up in Har - lem.

If you miss the "A" ___ train, ___

you'll find you've missed the quick - est way to

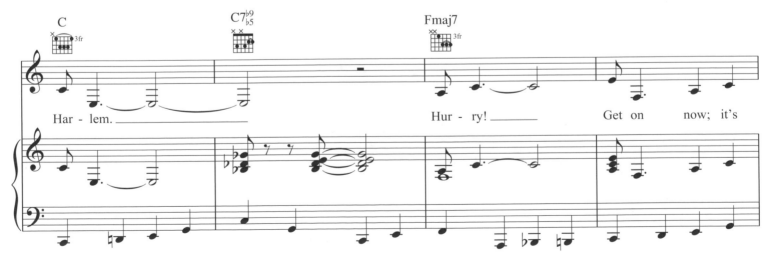

Har - lem. ___ Hur - ry! ___ Get on now; it's

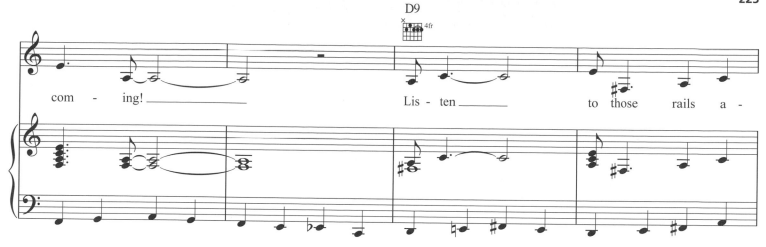

com - ing! _____ Lis - ten _____ to those rails a -

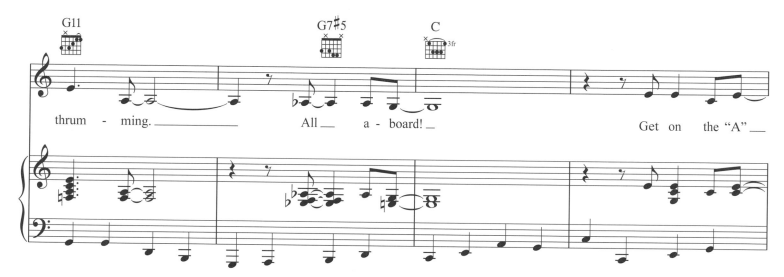

thrum - ming. _____ All _ a - board! _ Get on the "A" _

_____ train. _____ Soon you will be on Sug - ar Hill in

Har - lem. _____

D.S. al Fine

SWEET LORRAINE

Words by MITCHELL PARISH
Music by CLIFF BURWELL

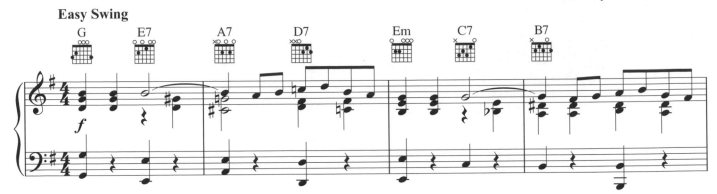

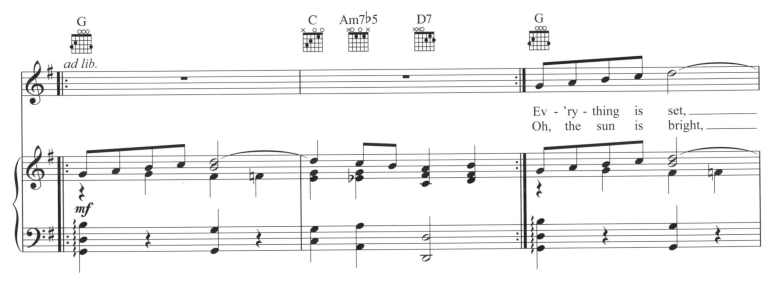

Ev - 'ry - thing is set, _____
Oh, the sun is bright, _____

_____ skies are blue.   Can't be - lieve it yet, _____   but it's true.
_____ life seems good;   For she said last night _____   that she would,

choo - choo toy, _____ when I'm with my sweet Lor - raine. _____ A

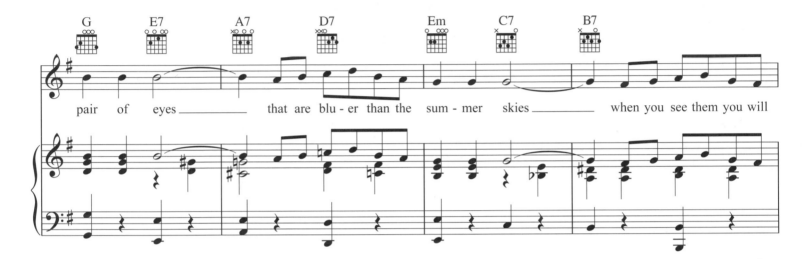

pair of eyes _____ that are blu - er than the sum - mer skies _____ when you see them you will

re - a - lize _____ why I love my sweet Lor - raine. (I'm so hap - py)

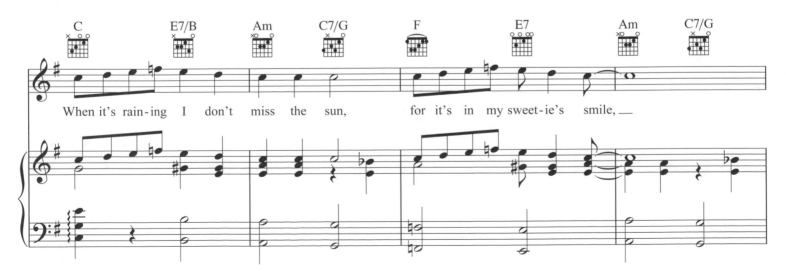

When it's rain - ing I don't miss the sun, for it's in my sweet - ie's smile, ___

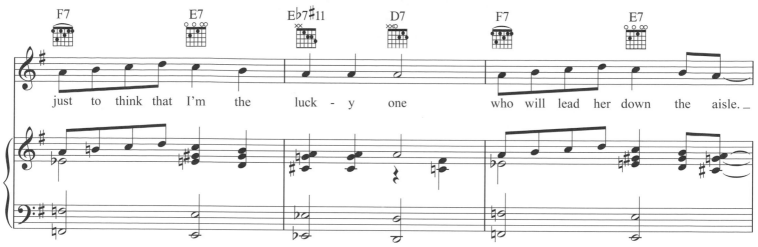

just to think that I'm the luck-y one who will lead her down the aisle.

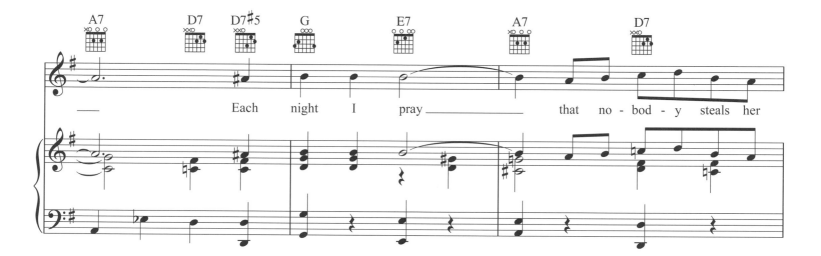

Each night I pray _____ that no-bod-y steals her

heart a - way. _____ Just can't wait un - til that hap - py day, _____ when I mar - ry sweet Lor-

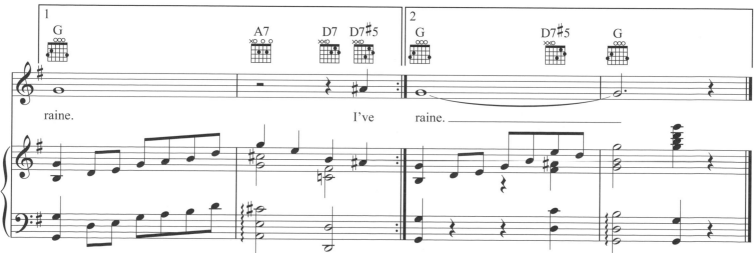

raine. I've raine. _____

TANGERINE

from the Paramount Picture THE FLEET'S IN

Words by JOHNNY MERCER
Music by VICTOR SCHERTZINGER

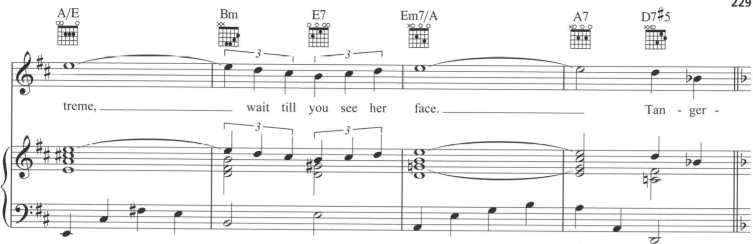

treme, _____ wait till you see her face. _____ Tan - ger -

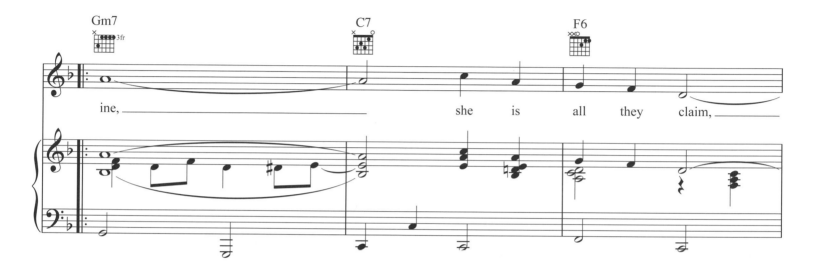

ine, _____ she is all they claim, _____

— with her eyes of night and lips as bright as

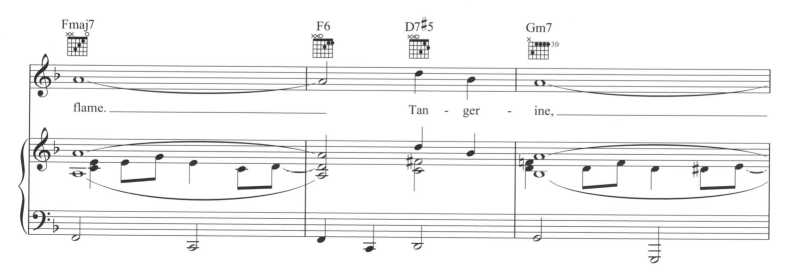

flame. _____ Tan - ger - ine, _____

when she danc - es by, _____ se - ño -

ri - tas stare and ca - lle - ros sigh. _____

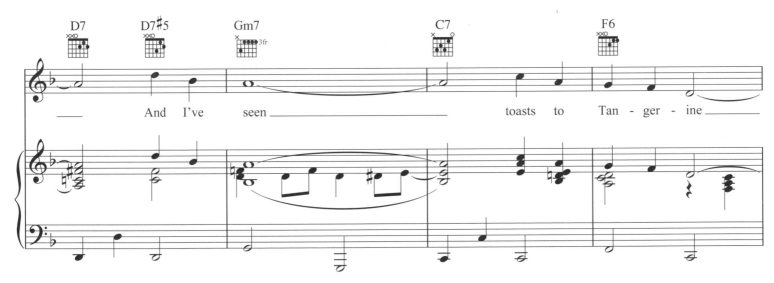

And I've seen _____ toasts to Tan - ger - ine _____

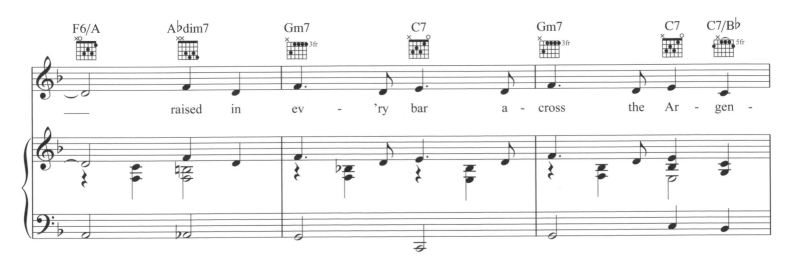

raised in ev - 'ry bar a - cross the Ar - gen -

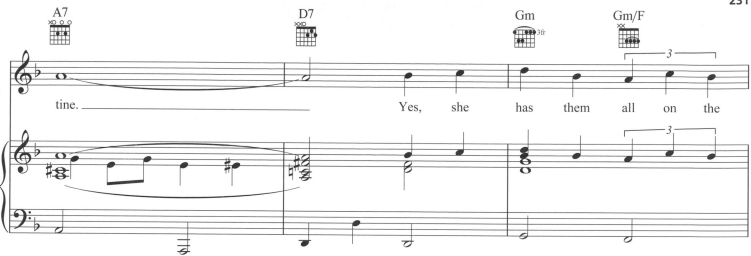

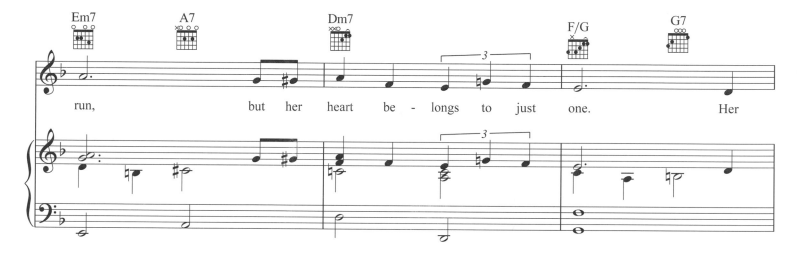

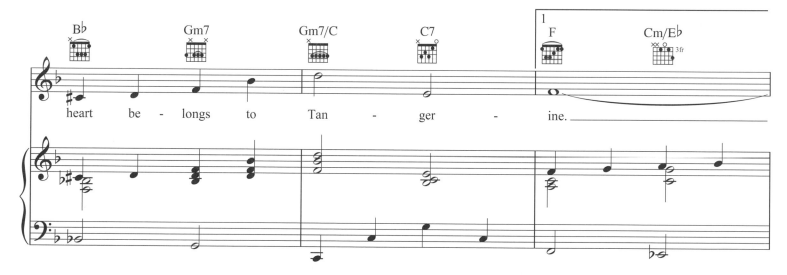

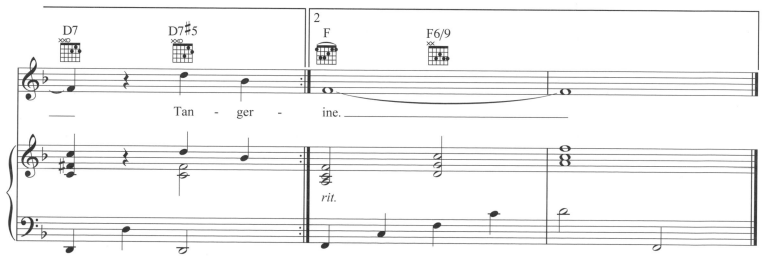

TENDERLY

from TORCH SONG

Lyric by JACK LAWRENCE
Music by WALTER GROSS

Moderately

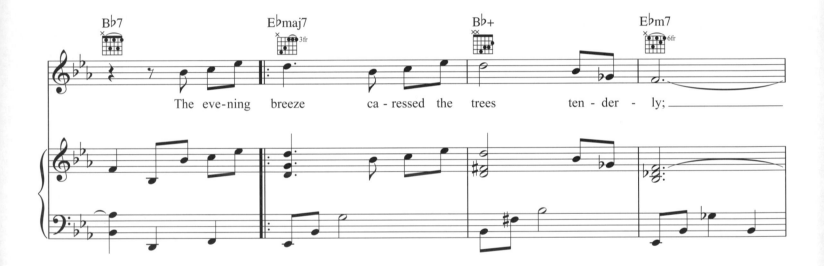

The eve-ning breeze ca-ressed the trees ten-der-ly; ___

___ the trem-bling trees em-braced the breeze ten-der-ly. ___

Then you and I came wan - der - ing

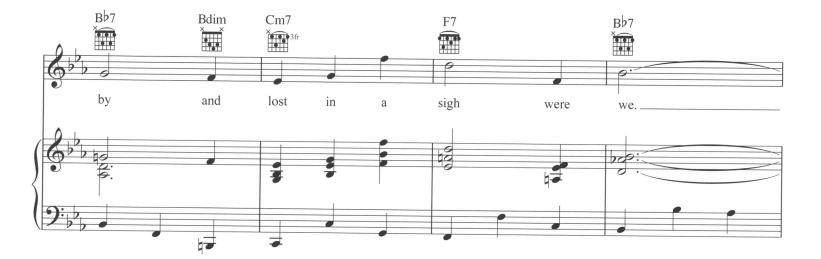

by and lost in a sigh were we. _____

The shore was kissed by sea and mist ten - der - ly. _____

I can't for - get how two hearts met breath - less -

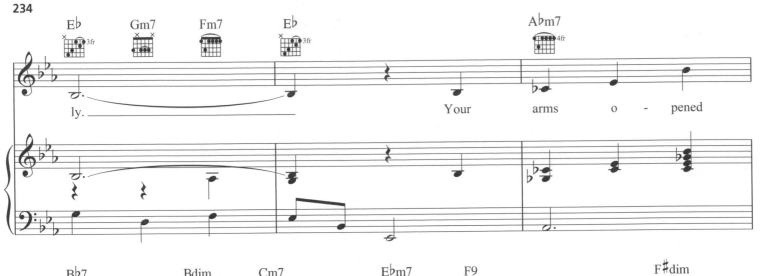

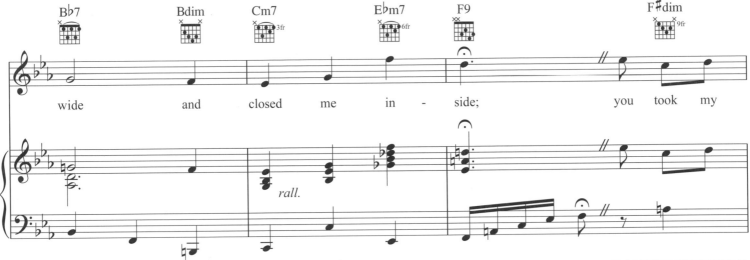

UNDECIDED

Words by SID ROBIN
Music by CHARLES SHAVERS

Moderately

It seems that you keep slow-ly

driv-ing me cra-zy.

I can't make head __

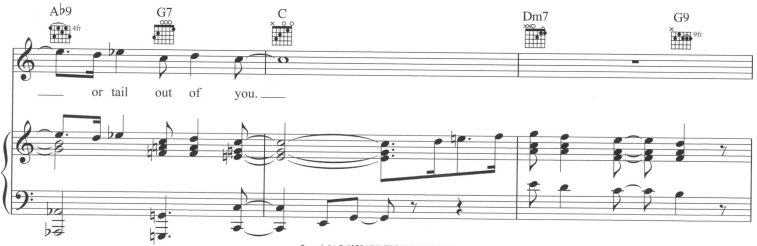

__ or tail out of you. __

My mind's gone bad. I feel ___ that ev - 'ry - thing's ha - zy.

Don't know ex - act - ly just what to do. ___

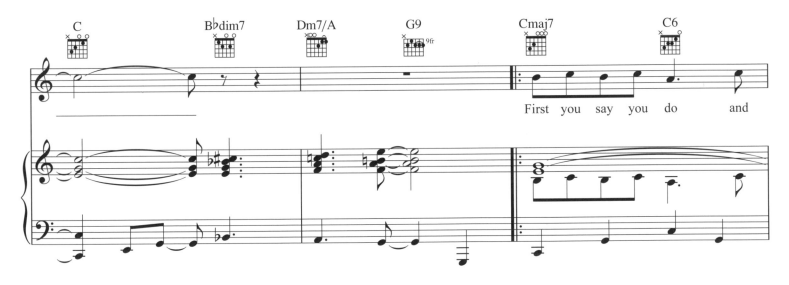

First you say you do and

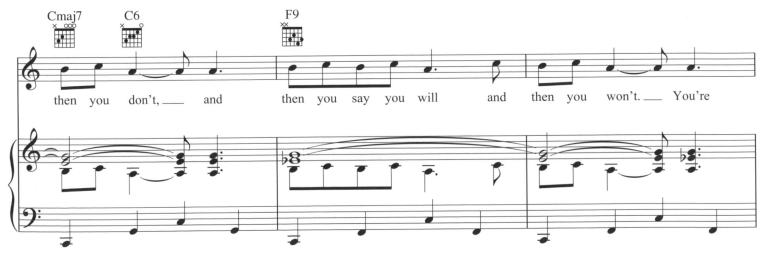

then you don't, ___ and then you say you will and then you won't. ___ You're

un-de-cid-ed now, so what are you gon-na do? _____

Now you want to play, and then it's no, _____ and

when you say you'll stay, that's when you go. _____ You're un-de-cid-ed now, so

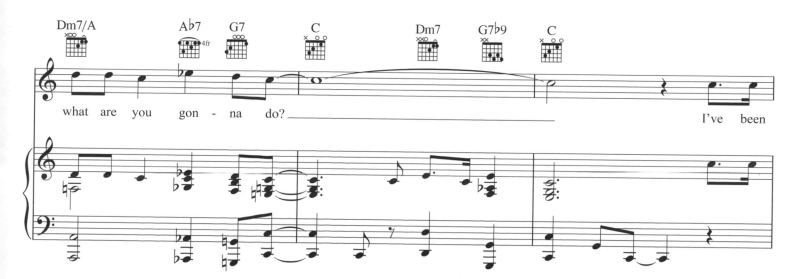

what are you gon-na do? _____ I've been

sit - ting on a fence, and it does - n't make much sense, 'cause you

keep me in sus - pense and you know it._____ Then you

prom - ise to re - turn, when you don't, I real - ly burn. Well, I

guess I'll nev - er learn, and I show it._____

TUXEDO JUNCTION

Words by BUDDY FEYNE
Music by ERSKINE HAWKINS,
WILLIAM JOHNSON and JULIAN DASH

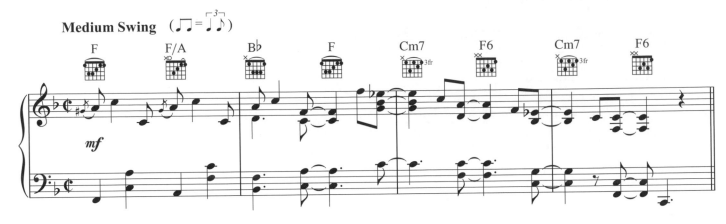

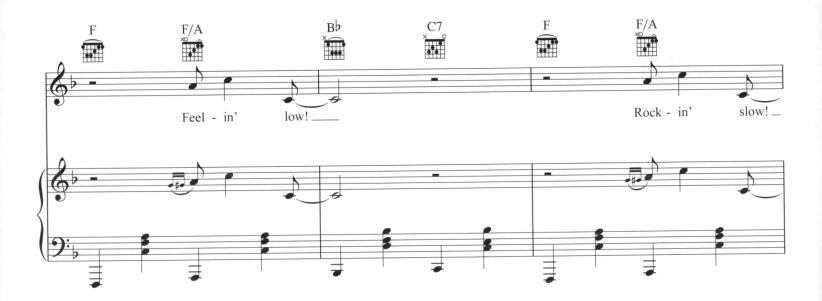

where I ___ be - long. ___ Way down South, in Bir -

- ming - ham, ___ I mean South in Al - a - bam's ___ an old

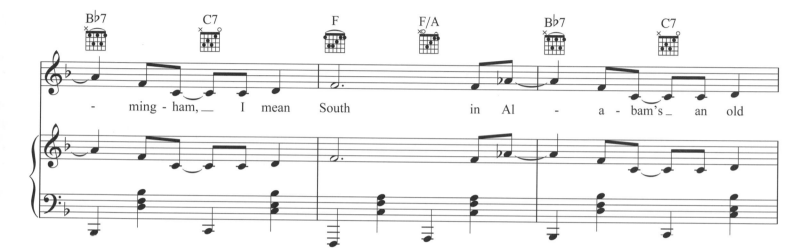

place where peo - ple go ___ to dance ___ the night ___ a - way. ___

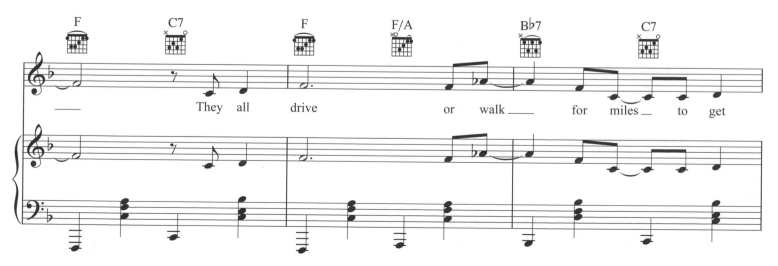

___ They all drive or walk ___ for miles ___ to get

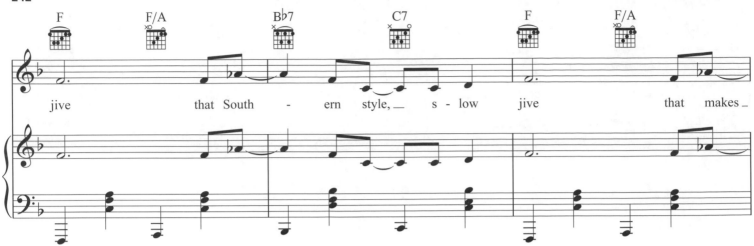

jive that South - ern style, __ s - low jive that makes __

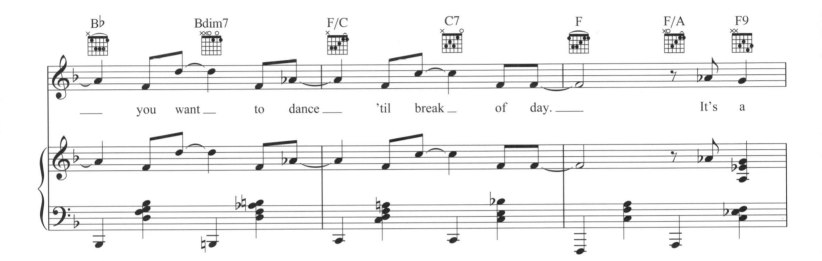

__ you want __ to dance __ 'til break __ of day. __ It's a

junc - tion where the town folks meet.

At each func - tion, in their

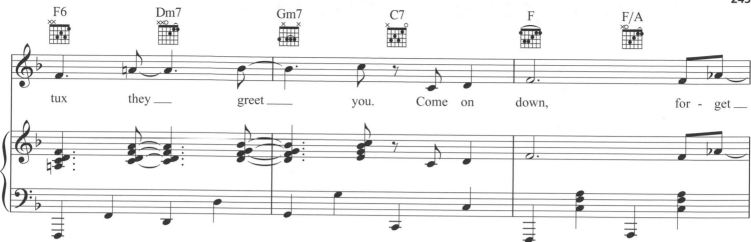

tux they ___ greet ___ you. Come on down, for - get ___

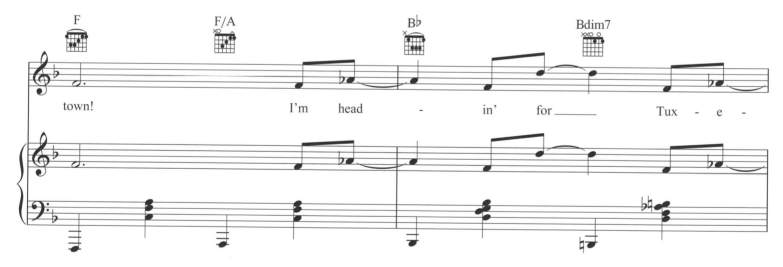

___ your care. ___ Come on down, you'll find ___ me there. ___ So long,

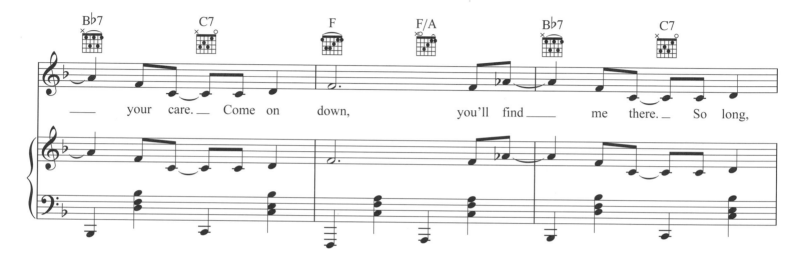

town! I'm head - in' for ___ Tux - e -

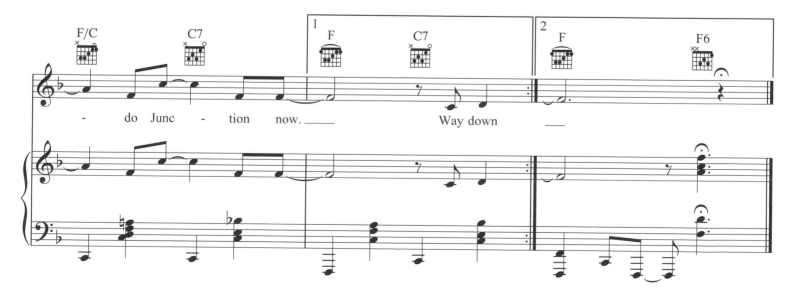

- do Junc - tion now. ___ Way down

WHY DON'T YOU DO RIGHT
(Get Me Some Money, Too!)

By JOE McCOY

Get out of here and get me some mon - ey, too. ___

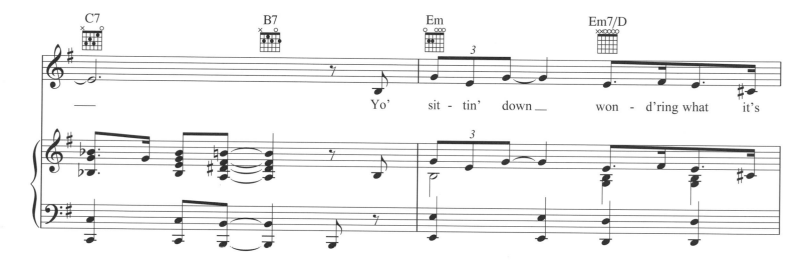

___ Yo' sit - tin' down ___ won - d'ring what it's

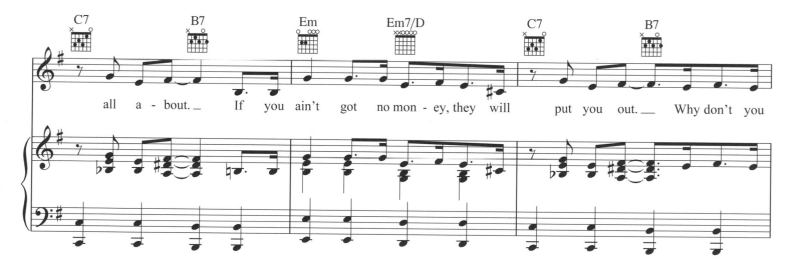

all a - bout. ___ If you ain't got no mon - ey, they will put you out. ___ Why don't you

do right, ___ like some oth - er men do? ___

Get out of here and get me some mon-ey, too.

If

you had pre-pared __ twen-ty years a-go, __ you would-n't be __ wan-d'ring now from

do' to do'. __ Why don't you do right, _____ like some oth-er men

WRAP YOUR TROUBLES IN DREAMS
(And Dream Your Troubles Away)

Lyric by TED KOEHLER and BILLY MOLL
Music by HARRY BARRIS

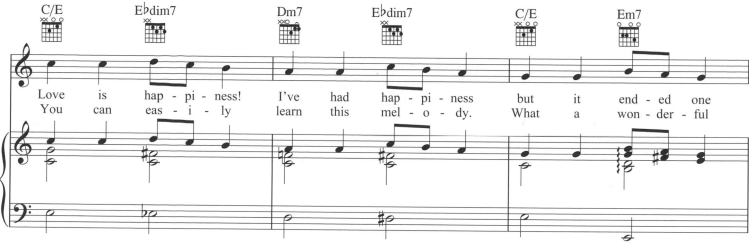

Love is hap-pi-ness! I've had hap-pi-ness but it end-ed one
You can eas-i-ly learn this mel-o-dy. What a won-der-ful

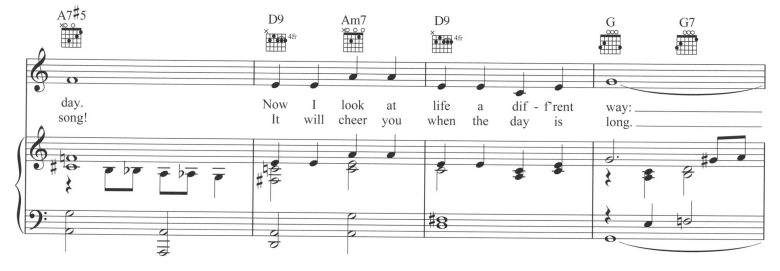

day.
song! Now I look at life a dif-f'rent way:
It will cheer you when the day is long.

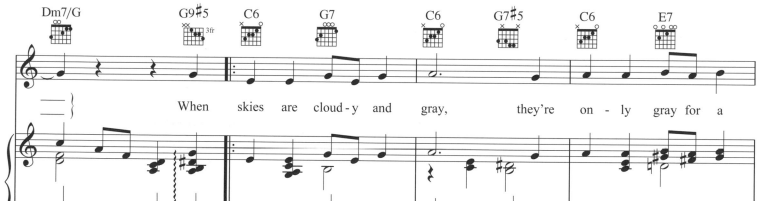

When skies are cloud-y and gray, they're on-ly gray for a

day. So wrap your trou-bles in dreams, and dream your trou-bles a-

way. Un - til that sun-shine peeps thru, there's on - ly one thing to

do: Just wrap your trou-bles in dreams, and dream your trou-bles a -

way. Your cas - tles may tum - ble, that's Fate, af - ter all; ___

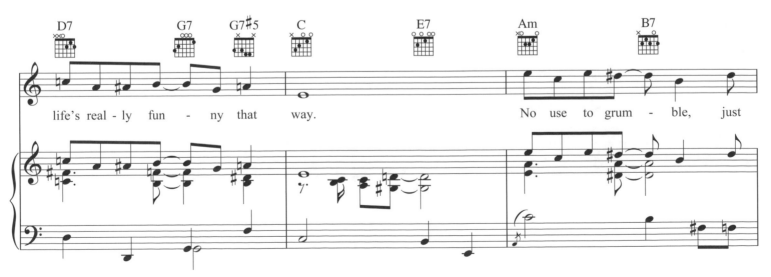

life's real - ly fun - ny that way. No use to grum - ble, just

smile as they fall. ___ Were - n't you king ___ for a day? Say!

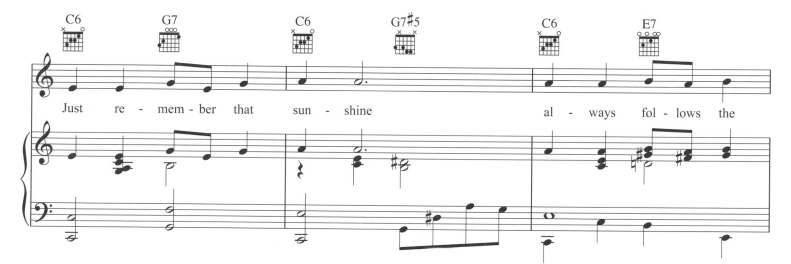

Just re - mem - ber that sun - shine al - ways fol - lows the

rain. So wrap your trou - bles in dreams, and

dream your trou - bles a - way. When way.

rit.

8vb

YES INDEED

Words and Music by
SY OLIVER

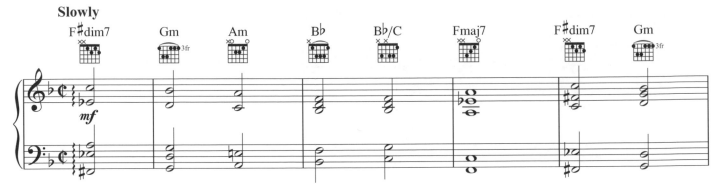

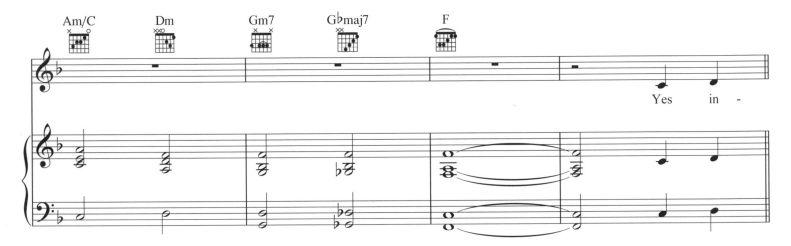

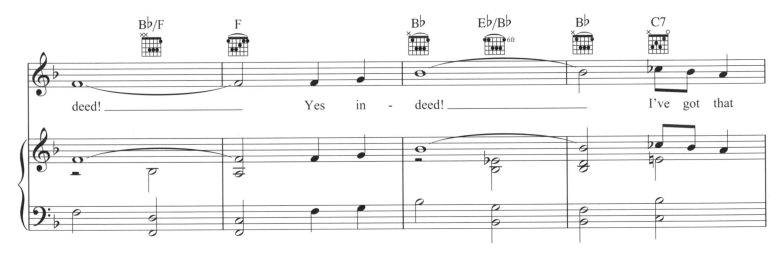

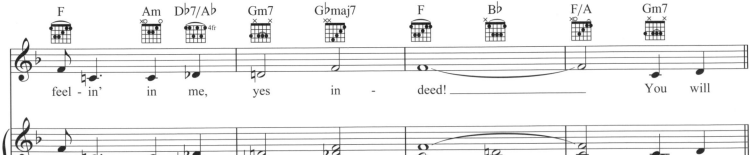

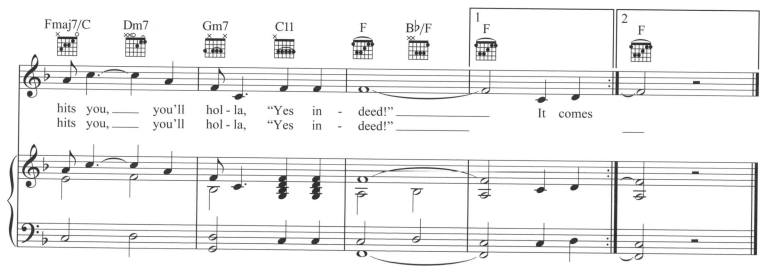

WHEN MY SUGAR WALKS DOWN THE STREET

Words and Music by JIMMY McHUGH,
GENE AUSTIN and IRVING MILLS

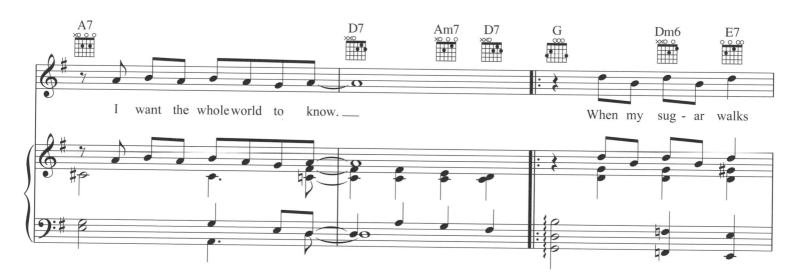

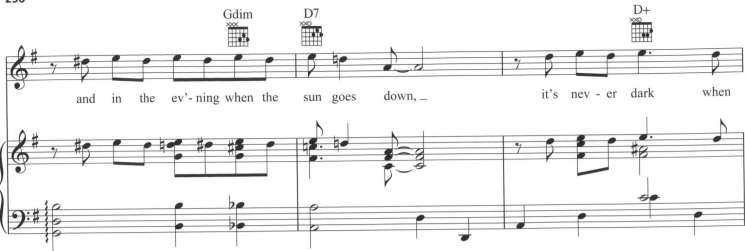

and in the ev'-ning when the sun goes down, _ it's nev-er dark when

she's a-round. _ She's so af-fec-tion-ate and I'll say this, that

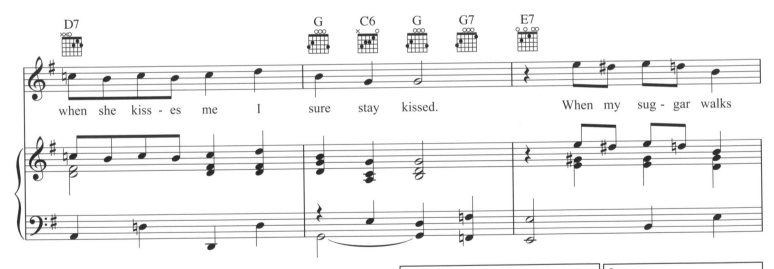

when she kiss-es me I sure stay kissed. When my sug-ar walks

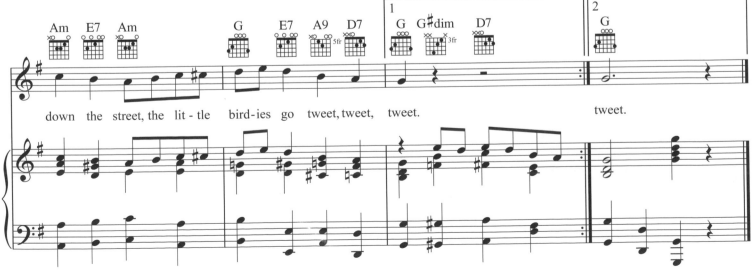

down the street, the lit-tle bird-ies go tweet, tweet, tweet. tweet.